God Sculptures
the Family

God Sculptures *the* Family

Myron and Esther Augsburger

National Library of Canada Cataloguing in Publication Data

Augsburger, Myron S.
    God sculptures the family

Previously published under title: How to be a Christ shaped family.
Includes bibliographical references.
ISBN 1-894710-10-X

    1. Family—Religious life. 2.Child rearing—Religious aspects—
Christianity. I. Augsburger, Esther II. Augsburger, Myron S. How to be a
Christ shaped family. III. Title.

BV4526.2.A93 2001   248.4   C2001-930714-4

GOD SCULPTURES THE FAMILY
Copyright © 2001 by Myron and Esther Augsburger

Previously published as: *How to be a Christ-shaped Family*
      by Victor Books/SP Publications Inc.
      ISBN 1-56476-073-1
2001 edition produced and printed by:
      Pandora Press
      33 Kent Avenue
      Kitchener, ON N2G 3R2

Song "Every Grain of Sand" on page 155 Copyright© 1981 by Special Rider Music.
All rights reserved. International copyright secured. Reprinted by permission.
Scripture quotations are from the *Holy Bible New International Version*®. Copyright©
1973, 1978, 1984 by International Bible Society. Used by permission of Zondervan
Publishing House. All rights reserved. Other quotations are from the *Authorized
King James Version* (KJV).

Cover sculpture: Togetherness, by Esther K. Augsburger
Photography: Robert Maust, Harrisonburg, Va.

International Standard Book Number: 1-894710-10-X
Printed in Canada on acid-free paper

10 09 08 07 06 05 04 03 02 01   10 9 8 7 6 5 4 3 2 1

Contents

Dedicated to
Caitlin and Lara,
granddaughters who
are loved

Foreword

I have known the authors of this book for over forty years. They are my parents, and I am very proud of them and their work in this book. As a practicing family therapist, I read many books on families, but I think this will always be my favorite — not just because it has been researched and approached with high ideals, but also because it is true to my knowledge of the authors.

While they draw from published family therapists and other theorists, their approach is intentionally not academic. Their writing is grounded in some of the basic constructs of professionals like M. Scott Peck, John Bradshaw, James Dobson, Mike Mason, David Augsburger, Merton and Irene Strommen, and others. And the greatest foundation for this book is the Bible. With scriptural support, they discuss the complex matrix of relationships and issues each family must address, from marriage to child-rearing, and through grandparenthood.

This book describes Christian families as sculptures in the creative hands of God. And each family, as each sculpture of an artist, is a unique creation affected by both its Creator and its elements.

The image of a family as a sculpture is illustrative of leading family therapists' views of the family as a system. Early and current leaders in the field, Gregory Bateson, Virginia Satir, Murry Bowen, Jay Haley, Carl Whittaker, and Salvador Minuchin, have developed and practiced a clear understanding of the family-systems model. Their model views each person in a family as a part within the whole system while remaining a distinct individual. The main principle of the systems theory is that the whole is greater than the sum of its parts. In other words, the elements of a system in combination do not just make up a collection, but because of the interaction of the elements, make up a complete whole which is uniquely greater. When you see a sculpture, you don't see a collection of metals, clays and stones; you see a single work of art.

Not only is a family a complete whole, but also a complex gathering of connecting relationships. Imagine, if you will, an invisible velvet rope tied from each member in a family to every other member. And the family is trying to cross a bridge. Their movements may each be different, some walking straight forward, some shuffling sideways, and perhaps some dragging along at the rear. They move along fine, as long as they all move in the same direction and within the range of the ropes. Now imagine one member stumbling forward. The whole family is not only jerked around, but each one changes his or her movements, in coordination with the others, to help the whole family regain its footing and maintain its balance. The rope between family members is the emotional connection of relationships. Because of this connection, each affects and is affected by others.

How the family system operates depends on its communication and understanding. In order to maintain balance as they move along, members are acutely aware of any tension or slack in the relationship ropes. The family develops unique rules for understanding these changes, and for coordinated balance and movement. All this is happening while each member grows and changes according to his or her own personal walk through life.

In the field of family therapy, many practitioners increase a family's understanding of themselves as a system by asking them to position themselves into a live sculpture. A few years ago our family participated in such a family sculpture during a large family reunion. This was such a memorable experience that it contributed to the inspiration for this book. The authors' family experiences and their vocations of Christian ministry and sculpture artistry combine to bring this metaphor to life.

One of my great pleasures in reading this book is in the stories, poems, and illustrations that bring color to the pages. Many of these are personal memories of life in our family. It is through these real experiences that one understands not only what the authors think, but how they lived their beliefs. And these became the foundation of their children's beliefs.

Myron and Esther Augsburger are masterful teachers, serious scholars, warm and caring human beings, and most importantly, dedicated Christians. Their writing style is deceptively simple because it describes complex issues in a way that is clear and straightforward enough to provide guidance. It is hopeful and inspiring. This book is honestly self-revealing and in it you will sense the love and understanding these authors have toward families, couples, and children.

Having read this book I can't say I know much more about these two. But then, I have known them intimately for four decades, and it is true to what I know of them. As simply as I know how to say it, this is a book you can trust.

John Myron Augsburger
Harrisonburg, Virginia

Introduction

When a sculptor creates a sculpture, the artist is not merely making an object like another recognizable object. Many different important elements go into the sculpture which are basic to its being a true work of art. It is like this with God, the Master Artist of all He creates. When God created the world, He structured the family by carefully designing it to be a beautiful work of art with meaning.

In creating a successful piece of sculpture, the artist must first be committed to putting him/herself into it. The sculptor must love the work and the work must reflect that love. Basic elements, such as the choice of materials, the tools used, and the method of working then are chosen to suit the nature of the intended sculpture. The fullness of the idea of the sculpture is accomplished when the artist creates a balance of unity, variety, and movement in the piece by use of color, form, space, and texture. God's sculpture, the family, is not unlike a sculpture created by a human artist/sculptor. So in the chapters to follow, we will consider the family, using these elements as metaphors.

A sculpture is a statement of meaning, of values, of vision. And a family is a statement of worth, of relationships, and of meaning. In a special sense a Christian family is a sculpture by the hand of God. A sculpture does not happen automatically but by someone's careful design. A family statement can be the expression of the Designer working in its members.

Our central social unit is the family, the place where our lives are molded, our personalities shaped, our values established, our faith inspired, and our sense of purpose extended. The better we can understand the inner workings of our own family, the better we can understand ourselves and our place in the family.

One of the more crucial units of society is the young family where parents are between twenty-five and forty years of age, when the clay which the Sculptor uses is soft, when the children are very young. This is the period in which the generation of tomorrow's leadership is being formed. It is the period in which families should be enjoying each other in working at the most exciting calling we have, that of being family.

In this spirit, this book is especially for young families, focusing on principles and elements that enrich their lives as couples, as parents, and as children. The family is at its best when modeling and encouraging each other to mature in the likeness of Christ, the ultimate model for the sculpture.

In the earliest years parents help young children to develop their personalities, providing a sense of love, security, and creativity. As children move from elementary to secondary levels of study, parents should help them to develop their ethical and moral values. Later, at the collegiate level the young person is working at interpretation and integration of thought. Parents are less direct and become basic sources of reference when children become young adults.

Sculpture is both a process and an achievement. It is dynamic in process and expressive in form. As persons, we are always in a process of becoming. In a real way we will be what we are becoming, and we are now becoming what we purpose to be.

Knowing that we were writing this book, Michael, our second son, wrote, "Dad always said, 'Family is where they know all about you and love you anyway.' Mom would give you her best haircut, and try to dress you with the nicest clothes she could get you to wear, and as she watched you go out the door to do your best she would say, 'Remember who you are.'

"That might have meant to remember where you come from, or that you are a part of this family; but in time, when maybe the chips were down, I would learn to remember who I was, with my own purpose and potential.

"About the time you would be in a fix with things so muddled up you couldn't see your way, Dad would be standing there with a finger toward the future saying, 'One's intentions for the future have more power to change one's life than all of the experiences of the past.' "

Our daughter Marcia wrote her comments as well, "I have had great difficulty choosing one thing to contribute to this book that characterizes our family development; there are so many. Having to choose one topic, I have chosen that which not only gives a family identity and cohesiveness but also gives individuals self-worth and connectedness. My parents made me feel that the most enjoyable times in their lives were those that involved our family. I recall my father canceling a meeting so he could attend my high school senior banquet, freeing his Tuesday evenings so he could take me skiing on "Budget Night," flying to California after his father's funeral, in time for the reception following my law school graduation.

"I remember my mother taking me camping at a lake one summer, making me a costume for a neighborhood parade, complete with a top hat made from a Clorox bottle. And I remember the look of love on her face as she pulled my baby clothes and stacks of cloth diapers out of a cedar chest when my daughter was born. I remember my parents taking us three children on what we thought was an afternoon outing, until we pulled into a motel and found they had packed bags for each of us so we could stay overnight to swim in the motel pool and get away from the phone to be together.

"Now, as a busy attorney, I find myself working fifty to

sixty hours a week, as my parents always did. Recently, on the eve of a complex trial, I visited my daughter's classroom to lead the second grade in music; my parents would have done the same."

As a couple with over forty years of enriching marriage and family life, with tensions and adjustments, making mistakes and forgiving, with joys and sorrows, with successes and failures, with love and painful caring, with ideals and disappointments, we, Myron and Esther, with our children, their spouses, and our grandchildren, find the family to be our most important and trusted circle of friendship. While sharing disappointments together, we love each other the more. When the Sculptor is having a difficult time crafting us into His image, we are confident enough in each other and in Him to believe that in His work we reflect His grace and glory.

In the early years of our marriage we shared in ministries in which we spoke to the values of family life. The danger then was that we might be idealists rather than realists. Now the danger in looking back and interpreting is that we may be revisionists rather than historicists.

Through his years of preaching Myron has often said that the long-term responsibility of parents is to make themselves unnecessary to their children. Together, we have experienced the change of relationship in which it is no longer so much parents to children, but rather friends to friends who happen to be the parents and the children.

Someone, before having a family, once wrote a book entitled, *Ten Rules for Child Training*. Later, married and with children, a second edition was entitled, *"Ten Suggestions for Child Training."* Some years later a third edition was revised with the title, *"Ten Hints for Child Training."* The last one is where we find ourselves. The chapters which follow will look at some things we as a family have experienced, as God is at work in us. We will be candid about the pebbles in the clay or the knotholes in the wood which make it difficult for the Sculptor; we will also share the

times that the tender hand of the Sculptor has reached into
our lives, for these far outnumber the pebbles and the
knots. We will look too at the guiding principles by which
the Sculptor works, as found in the Scriptures which He has
given us.

Myron and Esther Augsburger
Washington, D.C.
1994

Chapter One
God's Sculpture Makes Love Visible

Dear friends, let us love one another, for love comes from God. Everyone who loves has been born of God and knows God. Whoever does not love does not know God, because God is love (1 John 4:7-8).

If there is a place where the love of God is to be fully expressed, it is in His sculpture, the family. Life is to be enjoyed! God created us in pleasure, saying of creation, "It is good." The Scripture reveals that it gives Him pleasure to share with humanity.

Of Jesus His Son, God said, "This is My Son, whom I love; with Him I am well pleased" (Matthew 3:17). That God has pleasure in us is expressed in terms of fellowship, for Jesus said, "I no longer call you servants . . . Instead, I have called you friends" (John 15:15). Paul wrote, "The fruit of the Spirit is love, joy, peace" (Galatians 5:22), evidence that we are to live in the joy of love.

One of our greatest privileges is to model the love of the Divine Sculptor. And yet, in family we are so close to each other that we see our failures as well as our successes. With all of our love we are not blind to idiosyncrasies, to the pebbles in the clay, and to the failures which beset each of us. Our family relationship is not one of perfectionism but of enablement and faith in the good.

One of the basic elements in a work of art is color. There are what we call cool colors such as blue and green. Red, orange, and yellow give us feelings of warmth. Color can enrich a work of art or make it unpleasant to live with. Love is the warm color of family life.

In *The Road Less Traveled* M. Scott Peck, M.D. writes, "Ultimately love is everything."[1] Love draws us beyond ourselves, but it also, when genuinely experienced, expands and enriches our lives. Loving is not easy, for it must be constant, creative, and supportive.

Love is making room for others; it is transcending selfishness and independence; it is sharing with each other. Love, when authentic, relates without manipulation, shares without dominating, and enjoys without taking. Love is giving. But love is a risk, for it includes being vulnerable. Selfishness is inherent in our fallible makeup since the first woman and man partook of the forbidden fruit. We witnessed this selfishness in the actions of a young boy in a family we visited on a mission field, when at dinner he looked over the pieces of pie, licked his finger and touched the largest one, saying "That's mine!" Myron said he felt like licking his own finger, touching the same piece and saying, "You can have it."

Love moves us beyond our self-interests. It includes the well-being of another, even the pain and problems that a loved one carries. In love we are saying, "Your problem is now my problem."

> There is risk in love
>   in trusting oneself to another,
>   in trusting the other,
>   in trusting the dynamics of relationship.
>
> There is wisdom in this risk
>   in moving beyond the familiar,
>   in daring beyond the controlled,
>   in growing beyond one's borders.

There is excitement in discovery
in finding enrichment in others,
in developing abilities to share,
in bonding with new expectations.

There is wholeness in relating
in the fullness of the imago Dei,
in male and female relationship,
in love-covenant with one who is other.

The Meaning of Love

One of the principles in a work of art is unity. A good sculpture is not simply a conglomerate of individual parts. Each form within that sculpture should not be an entity in itself but must relate to all the other parts, for the sake of the whole.

To love means to seek identity with the other, to open one's life intimately to another. When Jesus was asked about the great commandment, He said, " 'Love the Lord your God with all your heart, and with all your soul, and with all your mind and with all your strength.' The second is this: 'Love your neighbor as yourself' " (Mark 12:30-31).

This text means that we are to open our total lives intimately to God: the *heart,* that is our affection; the *soul,* that is our ambition; the *mind,* that is our attitudes; and the *strength,* that is our activities. And to love our neighbor is to open our lives to what God is doing in our neighbor, be he a friend or an enemy! Intimacy with God enables intimacy with one another.

King Solomon spoke of the power of love to draw persons together:

Place me like a seal over your heart,
like a seal on your arm;
For love is as strong as death,
its jealousy unyielding as the grave.
It burns like blazing fire,

like a mighty flame.
Many waters cannot quench love,
   rivers cannot wash it away.
If one were to give
   all the wealth of his house for love,
   it would be utterly scorned.
            Song of Songs 8:6-7

A common cliché, "the family circle," is often used without any thought to the true meaning of "circle."

In the Western culture, the circle is a symbol of love. Thus, we exchange gold circles, wedding rings, at the time we make our marriage commitments. This circle of love symbolizes that love is infinite — never ending; it is continual and it is embracing. As children are added, the circle is enlarged and yet stays in an openness of acceptance and equality. As the family matures and relationships become adjusted in roles, a family sculpture can help us see whether those maturing relationships have equity, respect, mutuality, and love as integrating characteristics.

Personality patterns directly relate to the limits or freedoms in which a family celebrates love. For example, Myron's personality is more rigid than Esther's, perhaps more disciplined in terms of scheduling, and tends to be more private, even internalized. He is aware of this, and keeps seeking to develop patterns that are more "personable." At the same time he is more of a generalist, and less perfectionistic. Esther's personality is winsome and friendly, outgoing; she is disciplined in her achievements and somewhat perfectionistic in expectations.

Our three children have completely different personalities. Two of them are more openly expressive of their feelings. John, the eldest, is more introspective and expresses his feelings differently. From the time he could write any words, he would leave little notes to us on our dresser. Sometimes love notes, sometimes "I need you" notes. Each personality has its own way of expressing love.

One time Myron, while reading a book entitled, *Are You Fun to Live With?* asked our youngest, Marcia, who was quite small, "Am I?" She quickly responded, "Sometimes!" Children can be so honest. Our response to this honesty is a key as to how they will view our authenticity.

Family love and respect will also show up in the patterns of relationships children have beyond the family. We saw this expressed when John was in first grade. After he was tardy coming home from school several times in a row, his mother pressed him to know why he was late. John responded, "You know the little Hostetter girl?" And with his mother's affirmative response, for she knew that in the class there was a neighbor girl who suffered from a heart defect since birth, he continued. "She can hardly make it walking up the hill, she can't get her breath. So I take her on my back, and carry her to the top of the hill, and it takes longer for me to come up the hill." John was living out in his own quiet way what it means to love and care about others. Here was an opportunity for his mother to reinforce his loving spirit with praise. The little Hostetter girl died a couple of years later, and John's love for those who are hurting lives on. He is now a family counselor by profession, still reaching out to the hurting.

Freedom to Love

Maturing in the freedom of love is a steady and very demanding process. Each person needs to respect the others' particular characteristics, and at the same time grant the others space. In the process of maturing we have become more sensitive to avoid attempts to form one another in a given mold of preference.

This process of maturing in love must be a self-conscious effort. One of the enemies of family harmony is taking one another for granted, when we should enrich and respect and lift up the others. When our second son, Michael, was six, we had our third child, a beautiful little girl, Marcia.

Some months after her birth we went to visit their grand-parents. A next door neighbor, Walter, who was a pastor and knew our family well, began to tease Michael. He told Mike that they had a new baby at his house too, a little boy, who was cuter than Michael's little sister. He invited Mike to come and see his little son. As Michael took a look at his baby, Walter said, "Now, don't you think I am right? He is much cuter than your baby sister." Michael screwed up his face in thought, and said, "When my mother goes shopping, she doesn't just buy any old thing; she looks around until she finds the best, and then she buys it!"

Respect means that we must be consistent in the contin-ual cultivation and celebration of love. Tender expressions of love serve to create the highest respect and security in our relationships. Love is something that we do, not some-thing that we only feel: we share love, we express love, we cultivate love, we make love. Yet so often we are hesitant to openly express love, even with the simple words, "I love you." It is so important to tell our children that we love them and to tell each other as spouses, "I love you," not only when we are alone but in the presence of our children. One of the greatest and most important gifts we can give our children is to love each other.

Esther's father was a very warm and loving parent. How-ever, his strict German-Lutheran background conditioned his difficulty in saying, "I love you," or even in giving com-pliments to the children. Each of the four children are very sure that, as Esther says, "Papa loved us very much. He would sit beside our bed by the hour when we were sick. He would do special things for us, often when he couldn't afford it. He would hold us close while he told us stories in the evenings." She recalls that when the children returned from the Himalaya Mountain region boarding school which was 1,000 miles away from their home and involved nine months of the year, her Papa would hold them close with tears of joy. He would often hold and kiss their mother in front of the children. They knew how much he loved her.

And Esther says, "We knew Papa loved us. But I longed to hear him say, 'I love you' to me!"

Esther recalls that one summer when she was home from boarding school for the three months, she was helping her mother clean, and while dusting her father's desk she saw a letter he was writing to her brother. Her eye caught her name in the writing, and in curiosity she read part of the letter. Her father had gone to great length telling her brother what a joy it was to have her home, and related little things she was doing like singing while helping her mother and bringing laughter and joy. She remembers thinking, "I wish he'd have told me that, but I'm sure glad I read it. It makes my day."

One of the moving scenes in *Fiddler on the Roof* is when Tevye, the main character, comes in from giving his blessing upon the engagement of his second daughter, and he begins to sing the question to his wife of twenty-five years, "Do you love me?" She responds in amazement, saying that after twenty-five years of mending his socks and cooking his food he should ask such a question, and then turns it around, "Do you love me?" The scene closes with the two sitting together singing in duet, a response to the question of love, "After twenty-five years, it's nice to know!"

Love is proactive; it takes the initiative in expressing another's worth. To know that one is loved and to be able to express love is a unique aspect of humanness. Eleanor Roosevelt said, "The most important thing in any relationship is not what you get but what you give. . . . In any case the giving of love is an education in itself."

As you look at your own family structure, you may discover the need for a greater consciousness of wholeness in the family. This is the recognition that each part stimulates the whole, and that the result is greater than the sum of the parts. Yet in the structure of family, we often tend to be more brusque with those close to us, taking each other for granted rather than cultivating mutual respect and joy.

Families should express love to each other
    lest they be so nice and courteous to others
    and so abrupt with those they love,
so concerned with outer impression
    and so confrontive with their inner circle,
so expressive of anger to those who are closest
    and careful of words with strangers.

At best, perhaps, a compliment in rough form
    where extreme candor at home
    may be an evidence of trust,
where criticism of even minor matters
    may be saying that we care,
where emotional disturbance in disagreement
    may be saying, "You matter to me."

We must work to cultivate a more gentle spirit
    where candor can be considerate,
    can be expressed with gentleness,
where differences can be confronted
    and anger be with issues and not with persons,
where intense feelings can be matched
    with forgiveness that says, "I care and I love you."

In the routine of life we need to be reminded that love includes words, but it is much more; it is opening one's life intimately to another. Love in family is a celebration of one another, an affirmation of the deepest level of caring. Love is an emotion, and as such, it permeates the whole of our personalities.

Love gives to family members a sense of belonging, the security of worth, and the enrichment of spirit. The security of love is expressed by God Himself, as in Isaiah 49:16, "I have engraved you on the palms of My hands." What a beautiful image of the Sculptor's love. To love and to be loved expresses the greater privilege of humanness, of being persons who share the image of the Divine.

But love is more than an emotion. It also involves the intellectual and the volitional aspects of life. Love can be enriched by our understanding of the other, which helps us to open life beyond the self-interests that tend to dominate us, and then to communicate with the other, a key to enriching relationship. Love is volitional, for it is the act of choice that includes the daring of risk of trusting oneself to another. To be vulnerable is a choice.

Love is not learned by theory but by experience. Love is caught from earliest infancy by being in the arms of a mother or father whose warm embrace offers both security and a sense of worth. This security is significant in the development of personhood, for with security there is never a lack of identity, of being one who belongs. This is instilled very early in the baby as its mother holds it to her breast for feeding; and when she rocks the baby to sleep with the comfort of soft singing or humming, she communicates the feeling of security. Esther rocked all three of our children to sleep from the time they were born until they were several years old. She knew she was creating a habit for each child, but it was one she never regretted, for these were some of the most intimate and rewarding times each day. Another good thing about this habit was that it forced her to make time to hold, talk with, and sing to each child every day.

Love Is Celebration

Love is the celebration of worth, a valuing of the other. It is affirmation and mutual esteem of the highest regard for the other's value.

> The celebration of love
>   liberates us from self-centeredness,
>   releases us from privatism,
>   transforms us from individualism,
>   engages us for the common good.
> In celebration, it transforms.

Love is a celebration of belonging. We will never forget how we felt when we went to the hospital to see our several-hours-old first grandchild, Caitlin. We knew for months that she was coming and we began to love her then, but the moment we laid eyes on this tiny beautiful person, we began our celebration of love which will never end. Little Caitie is a part of our very blood and our lives. We believe that many grandparents celebrate love for their grandchildren even more than for their own children. It is not that we love them more, but that we celebrate our love more freely.

God created humanity in and for relationship with Himself, in and for community. We share this community with God as we extend it in the relationships of family in which we participate in love for one another. When we celebrate life at its heart, we celebrate loving and being loved. And this love is unconditional, always there, reaching out to see the best in the other; it is encouraging, winsome, supportive. Helen Keller, in her blindness, reminds us, "Keep your face to the sunshine and you cannot see the shadow." Love has a way of minimizing the shadows of negative feelings in our lives.

> It is an unpleasant fact, however, that most of our lives are governed more by our hates and dislikes than by our loves. I seldom know what I really want, but I know what or whom I deeply dislike and even hate. It may be painful to be wronged, but at least such wrongs give me a history of resentments that, in fact, constitute who I am. How would I know who I am if I did not have any enemies?[2]

This choice of being for or against is one of the special qualities of being human, of being able to discern and to choose. But we are first to be positive in our choices for God and His will, and then we can face the negatives correctly and know what to reject. Our focus is on the values that enrich rather than on the negations that seek to protect.

In conversation about the Gulf War, our friend, Senator Mark O. Hatfield, commented to Myron, "Americans don't know how to live without an enemy." We have in too many cases lost the spiritual values that can give us a common bond. Consequently, what we stand against in common becomes the force that binds us together. This approach is far too simplistic and negative. Jesus asks us to confront this defensiveness in life, to change our approach to one of love, a love that includes even our enemies. The spirit of love gives us a wholesome center of relationships, freeing us from enmity. It provides for us a course of positive action. Life with others, at its best, is a celebration of love. Agape, the God-given quality of unconditional love, enables us to love with constancy.

Love Enriches Values

There are three areas which are especially important to the Christian family, creation, culture, and redemption. As to *creation* we are involved in perfecting and interpreting nature, its development and use, its preservation and balance, its relationships and values. A sculptor reaches to the substance from the earth to transform it into a work of art. The material chosen determines the form for a successful sculpture. Its value is dependent on the compatibility of the material to the form, and the care with which the material is used. In God's sculpture, the family, we must recognize that nature is a part of the whole. We must see our responsibility in the whole scheme of creation.

We can build within the family a reverence for the earth. From the time children are very young, we can cultivate an awe and respect for the world God created for us to enjoy. When our children were very small, Esther was constantly pointing out the wonders of the colors of the layers of earth along the cliffs as we drove across the country, or the way the receding ranges of mountains change from darker to lighter by day and the opposite at night. She helped them pick up rocks and learn their geological names. She would sometimes put several dried navy beans between two soaking wet washcloths on a saucer for the children to check each day. The first day the little seeds swelled, the second day the skin was split, the third they could see a tiny worm-like sprout poking out from the split until the day they would put the new little plants into soil. Watching what really happens in nature gives the family a greater sense of value in God's plan. It also helps nurture a sense of responsibility for ecology.

Myron spent a lot of time with the children on the small, rocky farm at the bottom of the hill from our house. They grew up helping feed the few cattle we had as a hobby, watching calves being born, or buying calves or lambs from a neighbor to bottle-feed as a special project. One morning when Marcia was about eight years old, her daddy wakened her a bit early to allow time to check whether her pony might have had its colt. As they walked quietly down the still foggy hillside, they heard a light gallop at the bottom. As they stopped to look, out of the mist like the whisper of the wind, Taffy, the pony, went gliding by with a beautiful little colt close at her heels. An awesome and exciting picture. Marcia named the colt Misty of Dawn and called her Misty.

Not everyone is privileged to live this close to nature. But we all at times can see and be surrounded by the glorious trees and mountains which are for us to enjoy.

As Christians, we enrich the *culture* in which we share, not by idolizing it or being dominated by it, but by constantly challenging it and maintaining our integrity. Integrity means we appreciate the good and work toward change in that which is less than God's intention for humanity. Integrity means to enjoy and identify with our particular cultural characteristics, such as family eating our meals *together* (in some cultures the men eat first and children and women eat what is left), and celebrating girl babies as much as boys. Integrity also includes rejection of some very ungodly characteristics of our American culture—racial discrimination, materialism, and the search for fame.

As to *redemption,* we take the perversions of humanness seriously, always seeking the creative work of God's grace in correcting and building true humanness. This is especially true in relation to the many forms of addiction that beset the modern family: work addiction, sex addiction, alcohol and drug addiction, cigarette addiction, eating disorders, codependent people addiction, etc. We can teach our children that these things are "the little stones which weaken the clay" and even destroy it. We must be consistent in what we say and in how we react to others in the presence of our children.

One day Esther was standing in the bus station with our four-year-old Mike, waiting Myron's return from a preaching mission. A tall middle-aged man stepped up beside Mike, puffing on a cigarette. Mike looked up at him and said, "Sir, don't you know smoking cigarettes is bad for you?" He was dead serious and emphatic. Esther wasn't sure where to look or what to say, so she just looked down at Mike and smiled. Some parents would have reprimanded the child or apologized for his candid words and undercut all their teaching about respecting our bodies.

To help persons to freedom from life-damaging consequences in any of these areas is one of the present aspects of the kingdom of God. Our service as Christians is to enable persons to live by God's rule. Our mission in the family is to assist in the building of authentic humanness.

The family is in the business of people-making, of building each other, of being constructive and encouraging. We are persons in transition. There is more of life before us, and we are God's agents to each other in encouragement and development. Even in aging we need not cease to grow in different areas of life. As senior citizens we are to be expressions of the grace of God transforming life. There is now a politically correct term for senior citizens; we are the "chronologically gifted."

In the early years of our family, there were five of us in our family unit. We did so many things together. Very early, while we parents were in our twenties, during six years of intense evangelistic missions, we had a large tent with a seating capacity of over 5,000, and two tractor trailers to haul the equipment from one meeting to the next. We also had three house trailers for the team members. The staff lived on the tent grounds, almost as an extended family! Our family enjoyed these times together, as well as the enriching association with the other families in our team.

As the children grew older, we went hunting, fishing, boating, etc. together. Myron would occasionally take one son or our daughter along on a trip to one of his meetings. This made them feel special and helped cultivate the feeling of being an important part of the work. When they were older we took all three with us for speaking engagements in Puerto Rico. During lectures in California, we took the children on a two-week trip by auto to the west, the northern route going out and the southern route in return. A high point was the visit to Salt Lake City where Myron had conducted a citywide evangelistic crusade on the capitol steps for a week in 1963. In 1969 we took the whole family on a mission to Japan and India, followed by a trip around the world. We went to the Middle East, Switzerland, Germany, France, Holland, and England. However, two of our best summer vacations were when we rented a houseboat in upper New York for a week on the lakes and waterways. We were alone, away from the telephone, doorbell, speaking appointments, or television! We were afraid the children would be bored. But, to our joy, they loved it. We swam, fished, went water skiing, listened to tapes, and played games. Two years later, Myron cancelled a meeting in Brazil, and we asked the children what they would like to do for vacation. Their resounding response was, "Houseboat!" which we did again.

Later, when Marcia was in her early teens we took her along to Africa, and for a sabbatical in Switzerland including another trip to the Middle East. Later she accompanied Myron on a mission in Peru at a Wycliffe conference, and she and her husband also accompanied us to Guatemala.

We look back on the experiences and the monetary costs of those ventures as worthy investments in our family life. They were times of person-building, family-building, and bonding. Each of us will always have a global awareness of human need and of the relevance of Christian mission. In many ways our family has developed an international perspective on life, a benefit which they each affirm today. It has broadened our circle of love and enriched our values.

Virtue Is an Ingredient of Love

Family life together finds its security not in perfection but in the assurance that Dad and Mom love each other, and stand together even when they stand apart from each other on issues. It is this fidelity in love that communicates the values of the home, family relations, and of life itself. It is also the spirit of love which moves the values from the head to the heart where the values become virtues. As a consequence, those virtues are then lived out in children as well as by the parents. In the complexities of life, we often pursue these virtues with the stabbing pain of inadequacy and failure.

There are many aspects of this covenant to be fleshed out in life together. Living in love is still very much a living together in life. In wedding sermons, Myron has shared some of the following words of counsel:

> Be realistic, don't expect perfection.
> Be respectful of differences, don't demand agreement on everything.
> Be ready to forgive, never hold grudges.
> Be supportive rather than possessive.
> Continue to express affection for each other.

Compliment; never put the other down.
Develop commitments together.
Seek contentment rather than the pressure of
"keeping up with the Joneses." Slow down.
Always put "making a life" before "making a living."

Love is acting toward another in recognition of the other's worth. Love is caring, hurting when another hurts, suffering with another in problems, rejoicing in another's good, having lots of fun, and enjoying the richness of all of life together. We wanted to cultivate this while we engaged in the missions we shared. In one of the most beautiful pieces of literature found in Holy Scripture, we read:

> Love is patient, love is kind.
> It does not envy, it does not boast, it is not proud.
> It is not rude, it is not self-seeking,
> it is not easily angered, it keeps no
> record of wrongs.
> Love does not delight in evil
> but rejoices with the truth.
> It always protects, always trusts,
> always hopes, always perseveres"
> (1 Corinthians 13:4-7).

Love is giving the cup of cold water. It is hurting with others when they hurt. Our attitudes toward others in society begin with our attitudes toward each other in the family. This is expressed and caught in our prayers. Esther's mother helped form the lives of her family by having the children memorize the following prayer which they often said together at the breakfast table.

> Lord, help me live from day to day
>   In such a self-forgetful way
> That even when I kneel to pray
>   My prayer will be for Others.

Help me in all the work I do
   To ever be sincere and true
And know that all I do for You
   Must needs be done for Others.

Let Self be crucified and slain
   And buried deep, and all in vain
May efforts be to rise again
   Unless to live for Others.

And when my work on earth is done
   And my new work in heaven begun,
May I forget the crown I've won
   While thinking still of Others.

Others, Lord, yes, Others
   Let this my motto be,
Help me to live for Others
   That I may live like Thee.

                   —Charles D. Meigs

Thus the Sculptor's love is made visible!

Chapter Two
God's Sculpture Makes Trust Viable

Then the Lord said . . . "I have chosen him, so that he will direct his children and his household after him to keep the way of the Lord by doing what is right and just, so that the Lord will bring about for Abraham what He has promised him" (Genesis 18:17-19).

Let's paraphrase this verse in sculptural terms. "And the Sculptor said, 'For I have chosen this material so that it will create the kind of definition that will make visible the shapes and spaces which fulfill the idea that I want to express.' "

A piece of sculpture is a grouping of material which creates both positive and negative shapes. The negative shapes are always visually important. The sculptor uses the positive mass to define the negative shapes, those voids and spaces either within the mass or totally surrounding it. Without the positive mass, there is no definable shape — there is nothing, no meaning, no substance. The mass (solid material) is the frame of reference for the space to exist as shape.

God the Sculptor made a covenant with Abraham — and with us — to be that positive mass. We must trust Him to do the shaping so that the family will take form with meaning. God trusted Abraham to trust Him to shape him, so that God could fulfill His purpose.

God's self-giving covenant of trust is expressed in His sculpting of the family. His sculpture is a statement of togetherness, a shape of trust and belonging. It is a shape with open spaces, where arms outstretched to each other evidence the covenant which unites whole. Just as Abraham trusted his Father God to do His work and trusted Him enough to respond in faith by doing His bidding, so the parents in the family can trust. This is more difficult as the children grow older, because sometimes they follow the wrong bidding.

Children will be able to truly trust God if they can trust their parents. Children can be so unconditionally trusting. When Esther was a toddler, her father would stand her on the dresser or the stairs, hold out his hands and say "Jump and I'll catch you." She never doubted his word because he always caught her. He consistently kept his word. In fact she became so trusting that when a little girl no bigger than she came over to play, she told Esther to stand on the porch railing and jump and she would catch her! The let-down in trust was more painful to Esther than the broken bone.

God's covenant of trust is fleshed out in His sculpture, the family. The ability to make covenant is one of the higher levels of humanness. It is the declaration that one can think through values that are worthy of commitment, and then can make such a commitment with an integrity that can be fully trusted. When we are under stress or temptation, it is this covenant that brings us back to one another in love. In relation to our ability to share reciprocally in love, mutual trust is a foundational factor.

Rona Jaffe, a popular American novelist, sees marriage as we have known it as dying. She describes the changing of relationships from 'till-death-do-us-part, to "sequential monogamy." Well-known radio speaker for the family, Dr. James Dobson, describes the present pattern as "temporary fidelity." Covenant, when fulfilled in trust, will enable us to survive tensions, resolve differences, and grow together beyond cultural diversity. Mike Mason has written:

> We vow that we have had a visionary experience that will enable us to love "until death do us part." We have stood on the mountain, seen the new land, and become convinced that it is worth setting out for. If we stop loving before death, if we abandon the pilgrimage at any point, then what we will have done is to regress into a belief that there never was any mountain or vision of a new land, and that love is no enduring reality but rather a passing fancy, an illusion or a mistake or a matter of mere whim and emotion and circumstance. We will have shattered and rejected and invalidated one of the deepest spiritual experiences of our entire lives.[1]

When two people marry, they become bonded as one. The entering of covenant is central in the transforming of a friendship into a marriage. The two become one through the practice of covenant, of absolute trust. They are not made one by sexual union alone, but by the union of covenant.

A covenant of trust is not merely a contract. A contract may be broken and, if it is, either party may say it is no longer valid. But a covenant is the abiding faithfulness of each party to the other; and should one falter, the other is still there walking in covenant! As we mature in our "tryst," so we mature in our trust.

Trust in family is planted and nurtured in the children from their birth. The first indication of trust we noticed in our newborn son was when Esther undressed him for a bath. Instinctively he jumped and flung out his arms in fear of falling. All Esther needed to do was to gently lay her hand on his chest. He immediately relaxed. With this touch there was the response of trust.

The touch of God the Father transmits a sense of security and trust. Covenant is perceived correctly by understanding our relation with God. It moves faith from idea to relationship, moves behavior from discussion to action, moves spirituality from mysticism to discipleship. Covenant is the highest form of commitment that engages the human spirit. Trust is built on the reality of covenant.

One of the most important ways we experience this covenant of trust with God is when we pray. The family praying together not only engages us as persons with God, but also engages us together as a unit with Him. Prayer helps shape our lives together for meaning. In family prayer we are exercising our trust in God together.

One day when John was about five years old, he came to Esther almost in tears. He had lost his pocketknife and said that he had hunted everywhere. When Esther inquired about all the different possible places he might have left it, he moaned, "I've looked there." Then suddenly his face lit up and he said, "I think I'll pray and ask Jesus!" He buried his little head in her lap and prayed in silence. She sat there with some concern that he would be let down! As he lifted his head she saw the "lights go on" and he ran to the foyer, opened the clothes closet, and from the far corner of the floor snatched up the lost knife, squealing with joy! Oh, that we adults could have such trust in Jesus. It was simply God's covenant of trust with us in action. It could be nothing else, because we used that closet only for guests' coats and storage. Esther and John took time to thank God together.

A few days later Esther told this story to her father, who was such a godly and wise man. His response taught us an important lesson. He said, "Esther, I hope you didn't act surprised when he found the knife." He noted her questioning face and continued, "If we really trust God, why should we be surprised? Children aren't surprised when they tell you they need new shoes because the old ones hurt, and you take them to the store to buy new shoes, are they? Someone has said, 'We shouldn't be surprised at God's surprises, only grateful for the gift.' "

Models Are Essential

When Esther works on a sculpture of a human figure in a position of action, she needs a model to see which muscles are flexed, or what angle to sculpt the arm, or what direction the folds in the clothing take. Myron often becomes the model. God, the Sculptor of the family, uses parents as models as He sculpts the lives of the children.

The covenant between God and Abraham in Genesis 18 was built on the trust that each had in the other. This remarkable passage presents God as saying of Abraham, "I know him. . . ." This statement calls each of us to honesty before God, to stand in transparency before Him, and then to rest in the security of mutual trust.

In this text God expressed confidence that Abraham would teach his family the will of God. When we as parents share in such a teaching role, we will enable the family itself to become an interpreting community, interpreting the Word and will of God together, carrying its meanings into life. It is in the covenant community, family, and congregation, that the meaning of God's Word is discerned, interpreted, and practiced.

We as parents want to pass on to our children the heritage of interpreting the Scripture in context, and living under the authority of Scripture, rather than being determined by the patterns of the social orders of any time and culture. And this interpretation is not done in its fullness without a sense of spiritual community, of reciprocity between the spouses. Our children tell us today that they have no question about the sincerity and the integrity of our commitment to Christ. Fidelity is the one absolute necessity for a covenant of trust.

In our marriage we are both committed to fidelity to each other. Marriage is a covenant in which there is:

a reciprocity of fidelity and responsibility. The Old Testament views marriage as a covenant promise demanding fidelity of the wife; the New Testament stresses reciprocity in a world with an absence of such reciprocity. Its contemporary societies did not admit that a husband could commit adultery against the wife, but Jesus makes no difference between the two (see Mark 10:11-12).

The teachings of the epistles recognize equality in both rights and duties, require reciprocity in love and responsibility, and recommend mutual service and submission (1 Corinthians 7:3-4, 33-34, and Ephesians 5:21)[2].

The home is a place of covenant, and as such it provides for the child an atmosphere and a practice of trust. No place in society is more significant than the home for the expression and practice of trust. Even though they are immature, children should be held accountable to be trustworthy. This expectation should be first modeled by the parents, then taught and reaffirmed even when there have been failures.

A successful sculpture doesn't just happen. Creating a good sculpture is very demanding. It is not made as a leisure project, as a hobby. When Esther comes from her studio, it is evident that she has worked hard.

Building successful family life is a demanding commitment, but there are some clear guiding principles that help us. In their significant and extensive research, Merton and Irene Strommen have identified five "cries" or strong desires of parents:

Understanding
Close family
Moral behavior
Shared faith
Outside help

This involves the whole family, and as Merton and Irene Strommen in turn speak to family life, they interpret these five "cries" in relation to young adults as follows, "Our studies have shown that adolescents are vastly helped if they can draw on five great sources of strength:

> Understanding, affirming parents
> Close, caring families
> Moral, service-oriented beliefs
> A personal, liberating faith
> An accepting attitude toward receiving help[3]

As parents we must live by these values if we are to teach them, for they are caught in the manner and spirit in which we live in covenant, in which we trust each other. This is true first between parents, and then between parents and children. Parents who fail to respect and support one another, or who talk about each other in negative ways to the children when one of the partners is absent, destroy the very fabric out of which trust is woven. Such acts may be attempts by one or the other of the partners to gain an edge of control with the children, or they may be an evidence of immaturity, but they are actually self-defeating and destroy the climate of trust.

> Trust is extended,
> > as our respect for the other
> > as our recognition of fidelity
> > as our affirmation of reciprocity.

> Trust is earned,
> > as we evidence our integrity
> > as we authenticate our disciplines
> > as we engage each other accountably.

Trust is modeled in the way in which a couple adjust to one another's differences rather than trying to remake the other. Trust also enables us to transmit social values in an authentic way.

When Trust Breaks Down

The Christian fellowship in which we grew up taught us to believe that marriage is for life. When we married we knew that although there would be difficulties; these were to be seen as challenges for us as a couple to mature together. The community of faith would be responsible to surround us with the support, prayer, love, and counsel that would help us to achieve the adjustments necessary to be together as one, in life and spirit.

With the experience of divorce in our family, we have had to process together what it means to experience the breakdown of a marriage and the acceptance of a new person in the family circle. For us, as parents, it has been difficult to acknowledge and live with something that our convictions and ideals have so totally rejected—divorce.

But even in times of great difficulty, we have said to our children in love, "We'd rather have you with the problem than not to have you." And in this awareness we have come to a much deeper appreciation of God's grace, of His preferring to have us with our sin problem than not to have us!

In relation to our children it has not been easy to move beyond our own sense of loss, our grief at the violation of biblical ideals we hold to be so important, and to get beyond ourselves and enter into their sense of failure. We have had to learn to hurt with them and not just for ourselves, to participate in their adjustments to live beyond something that has died for them, a covenant which they had entered in a first marriage.

Too often as parents we fail to engage the feelings of our children who are directly involved in the problem—a betrayal of trust, feelings of failure, of rejection, of inadequacy, of social stigma, and of spiritual estrangement. Yet in empathizing with them, we have found new levels of understanding and appreciating the grace of God when we have so often betrayed His trust. Someone has said, "Pain is God's chisel with which He carves His image on the heart."

That divorce is wrong we all continue to agree in our family. For the breaking of covenant is an act contrary to both the will of God and to the highest in human commitment capacity (Matthew 19:3-12). We know the meaning of Margaret Atwood's statement, "A divorce is like an amputation; you survive, but there is less of you."

That divorce is not the unpardonable sin we also agree. We have come to see not only the possibility but the importance of a new covenant to go on with the one life God has entrusted to us. Further, as we read the Scriptures carefully, while God condemns all kinds of immorality, in relation to marriage he particularly condemns the violation of covenant and calls it adultery. In fact, adultery is expressed in German as "marriage-breaking," covenant-breaking. (See Matthew 19.)

In a second marriage following divorce, the new covenant is entered with the full recognition of the adultery that was committed in the act of having broken covenant. The meaning of adultery is not primarily in the sexual relation (as though this is to be "living in adultery" or committing adultery over and over), but is in the adultery of "covenant-breaking." This is something in which each partner participated as a sin in bringing closure to a covenant that was meant to be for life (1 Corinthians 7:2-6). Yet we believe that in a repentance which takes God's attitude toward this rather than rationalizing it, there is a grace of forgiveness and the creation of a new formation of social and family accountability.

We enjoy our family. We share together the joys and love of family life. We enjoy the wonderful memories of our years together in the intimacies of home and family sharing. We also share in mature love the pain experienced in working through the changes of broken relationships and the joy of new partners in the lives of our children. In these situations, we have needed to express the kind of love, grace,

and acceptance quite other than what the comforts of legalism would have sought to secure. We stand together in the
framework of God's love and grace as He accepts each of us
on grounds less than what His laws have asked. As Jeremiah
witnessed when he watched the potter, God can destroy
soft clay, renew it, and begin again to form the work of art:

> This is the word that came to Jeremiah from the
> Lord: "Go down to the potter's house, and there I
> will give you My message." So I went down to the
> potter's house, and I saw him working at the wheel.
> But the pot he was shaping from the clay was
> marred in his hands; so the potter formed it into
> another pot, shaping it as seemed best to him (Jere-
> miah 18:1-4).

Esther is also a potter. Persons watching her working on
the potter's wheel marvel at how easy it looks. They "oo"
and "ah" over the seemingly beautiful pot that quickly
emerges from the lump of clay. But sometimes they cry out
in consternation when she suddenly stops the wheel and
mashes the vase into the lump of clay with which she began.
Her hands were so sensitive that they could feel the flaws in
the structure she had just made. There may have been a
stone in the wall of clay, or an air bubble, or there may have
been too much thickness of wall on one side or another
which would eventually crack the clay when it was fired. At
that stage of the process it could not ever be useful. However, by destroying the shape immediately and removing the
stone or air bubble while it was soft, she could pull up a
perfect and beautiful vessel.

Only with God the Master Potter can the soft clay, which
has been full of stones, be reshaped into a perfect marriage vessel. The reason so many marriages don't hold
together is because the Potter has not been allowed to re-
move the stones before the clay has been hardened in the
fires.

There are many books available to help couples work at sustaining their marriage. Many of these are from persons with a Christian worldview, but there are also some very helpful books from secular sources. One significant work is *Passages of Marriage,* coauthored by Dr. Frank and Mary Alice Minirth, Dr. Brian and Dr. Deborah Newman, and Dr. Robert and Susan Hemfelt (Nelson). In this book the authors identify five stages of love in marriage: Young Love, the first two years; Realistic Love, the next seven years; Comfortable Love, the next fifteen years; Renewing Love, the next ten years; and Transcendent Love, from the thirty-sixth year on. This analysis is helpful for us to understand ourselves as partners, and to accept our "passages." We believe that forty years of marriage have brought us to the best times of all.

Karen S. Peterson, a reporter for *USA TODAY,* shared an interview with Michele Weiner-Davis, a marital therapist from Woodstock, Illinois, who is known as the "divorce buster." Weiner-Davis says that divorce doesn't solve the problems it purports to, that the majority of problems are solvable in solution-oriented therapy. Emphasizing solutions, a present and forward look, she says, "When couples spend too much time looking back and don't get solutions, they feel hopeless. It is hopelessness that dissolves marriages, not differences."

In her emphasis on staying together and working through the problems, she cautions, "Don't get hung up on the myths that can undermine your marriage:

> "Our problems have lasted so long, it's too late to change." This assumes that the partner is responsible for problems. Take control; change what you can.

> "I'm not happy because my spouse doesn't satisfy my needs." Happiness comes from yourself, not your partner.

"I can't put my happiness before my children's." No time for self means a dissatisfied parent and spouse.

"We can't communicate." Even not talking is a form of communication. Acknowledge and respect your different communication styles.

"We've grown apart." Actually, you've both probably changed less than you think; you need to rekindle what worked in the past.

"My spouse had an affair; it's over." Marital crisis can be an opportunity to renegotiate the marital bond and recommitment."[4]

Myron and Esther came from two very different cultural backgrounds. In our life-development prior to marriage, Esther was born and grew up in a jungle village in India in a large bungalow with many servants, and was educated in an elite British boarding school in Darjeeling, in the Himalaya Mountains. Myron grew up on a farm in flat northwestern Ohio, milking cows and hoeing weeds in the melon field with his dad and brothers, going in his first years to a one-room school, later working with his dad in carpentry work and painting. He was a part of a rural Mennonite church where he was nurtured, encouraged, and loved. Our adjustments in our marriage called for respect for one another's cultural heritage, and an understanding of factors that made us each act or react in different ways. Myron had to learn to like olives, and Esther had to learn to like rivel soup. Neither liked tapioca, so they were spared on that!

On returning to the States, Esther was at first fearful of fitting into the more parochial life of the church communities. As Myron matured he was equally fearful of fitting into the social patterns of society. He now jokes of early years of his ministry; at social dinners in his ecumenical preaching missions, he would continue visiting with the persons seated next to him until he could observe which of several forks to use first!

But in the adjustments, as a couple we have worked at mutual support and social and spiritual enrichment, with the resultant growth for both of us. Each has been able to trust the other to make them "look good" in settings strange to them. The longer we are married, the oftener we find ourselves anticipating an upcoming possibility of embarrassment. One of us will save the other from this by carefully interrupting what is on the verge of being said with something which saves the mistake from happening.

Family Life Is Togetherness

Togetherness is more than spending time together; it is actually participating together in common interests. As our family grew together, the nature of our work in Christian ministry in interchurch evangelistic missions and in educational administration and teaching did not easily lend itself to engaging the children's participation on their levels of development. This was especially true when they were in their preteen years. As we look back at this with regret, it has made us more conscious of the special difficulties associated with administrative and professional roles in the church.

This is a very real problem for many professional couples. The stress does not simply affect the respective spouses, as they each carry the responsibility and enjoyment of their individual roles; it is especially crucial in the lives of the children who are not a part of their parents' day-to-day work and who consequently may miss the privilege of being participants who are mentored in their development. This is why it is important that we as parents create a sense of partnership in the family by letting the children know that our success is dependent on the whole family, that the children are important to us in everything we do, whether they are directly involved or not.

Esther's parents, who were missionaries in India, always made their four children feel that they were also a part of the work. They were a missionary family, and their parents made it fun. So when they were at boarding school 1,000 miles away, they were still a part of the fabric of being missionaries. Life was not easy, but her parents never complained about the hardships and so the children didn't learn to do that either. To this day none of them harbor resentments toward their parents and their childhood like many of their colleagues.

When the children were all home from boarding school for three months, the family would pack their things and head for remote areas where people have never seen anyone outside of their village, let alone heard the name "Jesus." Esther, her mother, and younger brother would ride the ox cart, and the two older brothers and her father on bicycles would go ahead of the caravan of carts which carried tents, food, and helpers. Her parents made their work an adventure that involved everyone. All the children still talk about these experiences with excitement. They couldn't take toys along, so they were encouraged to be creative and make toys and games out of fallen green fruits, sticks, leaves, and stones. This was perhaps the beginning of Esther's sculptural pursuits.

Myron's background on the farm gave him practical experience close to nature. But one of the greater strengths was the way he worked with his parents, from farm work with his dad to work around the house for his mother. His parents were mentors in industry and thrift.

As families we need to creatively find projects in which we all *work together*. Most parents find it easier to become involved with their children in play. This is good. But it is also important to do some work together over and beyond the individual family member's routine chores. There is much which can happen in the child's self-image and value development when he/she works along side of Mom or Dad who is doing the same thing. For us as parents it would be much easier to do it alone, but involving the children is very important.

We need to provide ways to *be creative together*. No human being should ever say, "I'm not creative," for this is denying a very important element of being made in the image of God. One of the special things about us which other animal beings don't have is creativity—the ability to make and do things beyond mere functional purposes, things with meaning. It is important to help our children understand this by guiding them use their imagination in making things.

When our children were small and thought they were too big to take Sunday afternoon naps, Esther would pile paper (not coloring books—they don't require much creativity, only skill) crayons, scissors, and paste on the living-room floor, help them get started, then stretch out on the couch and blissfully relax, watching and napping in between answering "how to" questions occasionally, while the children quietly built three-dimensional towns with houses, cars, gas stations, and stores out of the paper. The week following they would transport their towns outdoors and play "little people" with their cousins who lived next door. Ants were their "little people." Sometimes it is good to simply be present when the children are playing. And sometimes they need to be on their own to create.

There were special things we did as a family, perhaps in compensation for Myron's absences in administrative work and in his many meetings in the wider church, which did enable us to spend time together. Regularly, when Myron would return from being away, the family would take a couple of days at nearby Natural Bridge with its motel and indoor swimming pool, with no one knowing where we were. We swam, hiked, and played games. Sometimes we spent several days with the Himes family, whose children and ours were close chums, at a mountain cabin playing, swimming, and fishing.

Occasionally, in Myron's absence, Esther and the children

would rent a camping trailer, hitch it to the car and spend a few days beside Todd Lake. John and Mike, who were in their early teens, pitched in as the men of the house, to crank up the top of the trailer, and to build the fire, while Marcia and Esther made the beds. All four prepared the food, went swimming and fishing, and played games by lantern light. On a number of Christmas breaks Myron would take the family to a hotel in Washington, D.C. for a weekend of sight-seeing and swimming. The goal was to be certain that the times together reinforced the trust levels of our love rather than to allow absences to create insecurities. In many ways we grew as young parents with our children and became and continue to be best friends.

Give Trust, Not Shame or Guilt

Trust is important in the development of identity. There is a direct relationship between expressions of trust and personal security. When we assure our children of our confidence in them by our attitudes and behavior, their self-image is strengthened.

We should not use shame or guilt to try to control a child's behavior. The experience of guilt is in many ways more common to Christians than shame. Guilt is a sense of accountability to a standard, while shame is the feeling of being rejected by persons. A guilt culture is directly related to monotheism and the resultant accountability to a personal God, while a shame culture is more often related to polytheism, with accountability to a social group. As society has less and less religious orientation, we will doubtless move more into the mode of a shame culture.

A person should see legitimate guilt as a call to live up to one's potential, and not allow it to be defeating. A guilt culture has an inherent problem of legalism. Shame has a positive and a negative side as well. On the positive side it holds the person to the values of the community. On the negative side it will often stifle the person by inhibiting him from functioning freely before others, and motivating him to "save face" at almost any cost. It can also create a serious inferiority complex. One of the most costly things to children is to shame them at all, but especially in public.

Shortly after Myron took office as president of Eastern Mennonite College and Seminary, Marcia entered first grade. A professional counselor told us that Marcia's teacher had a problem with any symbol of authority. So, when Marcia stood in "show and tell" time and announced that her daddy was just elected to a local bank board, her teacher punished her in front of the class for bragging. Our daughter told us about it with heartbroken tears, saying she told that because she didn't want to brag that he was the president of a college. This incident, along with some other ways the teacher shamed Marcia, gave her problems for years to follow.

Shaming another is one of the most devastating and lasting weapons a parent can use. It is a convenient way to cover one's own failures or lacks. We have all heard mothers in the supermarket screaming shaming words to their child; what is apparent is that they are trying to make an impression on others and save their own face.

Our two sons had similarly painful experiences because some people didn't know how to accept their parents' leadership role. One adult, perhaps partly teasing, would tell them that their dad's car was no good, that his was much better. For five- and six-year-olds, this was something to be ashamed about.

Even in high school, occasionally teachers would shame them by saying, "Just because you're the president's kid doesn't mean you should have privileges!" They still talk about some of their "shaming" before others. There are many different ways in which we can make another feel shame and cause much pain and damage. We should try to prepare and guard our children from such thoughtless incidents.

One of the tragedies of divorce when there are children is that it places upon the child the weight of answering for the parents' failure. This imposes on the child self-guilt and the need to "save face." For the couple, while there may be cases where divorce is the lesser of two evils—what Mason refers to as "a preferable hostility, and actually (in his opinion) a more acceptable one to God, than the continuance of a marriage in the face of chronic and unresolved bitterness"[5]—the children must also process honestly the problems that led to the divorce. One can't just walk away and close the door and be at peace. Divorcing parents must at least work through the healing of memories and shame together with their children.

In counseling people in our pastoral work, we have found that a factor not often taken seriously is the way in which persons engaged in a divorce tend to close the door on all of their past, without working through their responsibilities and ownership for their past problems. This blocking out of the past also closes the door on the many wonderful things that have shaped their lives. Mason gives us a very significant statement that relates to this:

> That is what is so distressing about divorce: it separates the divorcé not only from his mate, but in many ways from his own religion. And this tends to be true, oddly enough, no matter what sort of religion a person happens to hold. Even a religion of pure self-seeking and hedonism runs aground on the tragedy of divorce. The popular modern notion that partners can separate amicably, and even be "better friends apart than when they were living together," is a preposterous myth. The very fact that separation takes place presupposes unpleasantness and hostility.[6]

We sensed this kind of hostility and separation from the past in one of our children who went through divorce. One day Esther remembered all the hundreds of slides we took while the children were growing up. (We took slides rather than prints in those days, slides the family hadn't looked at for years—perhaps had never seen some of them.)

Esther felt a need to refresh her own memory of all the wonderful and happy times we had together. As the two of us retrieved the slides from our attic, we were fearful they had turned dark and faded with age. To our amazement they were fine. So we spent hours of laughter and tears as we looked at each of the slides one by one. Then Esther got a better idea—have them made into prints for each of the children and give them each an album of photos from their birth to graduation. Each album would include all five of us.

What a project! It took a lot of time and investment, from getting the prints made, pasting them in albums, to writing either something to identify a picture or a funny comment. But it was fun. We will share part of what we wrote on the first two pages:

> Photos not only enrich our images, but allow us to reestablish contact with those which have been lost to time. Images in our past influence our current view of ourselves and of each other. They can give us a healthy identity.
>
> Each photo in this album captures a special moment—John's first day off to school, Mike's big "catch-of-the-day" on the houseboat, a beautiful baby girl joining the family which is filled with pride in her, or the three of you in a rickshaw in India! They are landmarks of a particular period of our lives.
>
> Another aspect of identity which a photo album like this involves is our values and ideals. Often what we do and how we do it reflects such things as the importance of educational, occupational choices, selection of a mate, our global concepts and above all, our faith in Christ. Peer influences, experiences in society, and the need for personal ownership of

these things begin to change our lives from the adolescent stage into adulthood, but these values and ideals are rooted in the family. While the new structure is for each person unique and personal, it still includes the earlier influences of our lives. For example: our trips to developing countries have had their impact on our value systems. . . .

Another component of our identity has to do with each of our interests—our work, our play—where we are willing to expend our energies and investments. . . . It's sort of neat to look at these photos and make wonderful "connections" with our past.

This album can be a window of the past which can bring a more meaningful present. We hope that each of us, in looking through this window, can feel a good and healthy "me-ness" and the same time a sense of belonging to the "us." We also hope this helps us keep an identity with the Faith which has been the framework of our family structure and activities.

Our mission as parents is to impart values to our children so that they will own them for themselves. That a child can carry out the disciplines and live by the standards which he or she has been taught is shown in a beautiful story related by Harry Covert from Alexandria, Virginia, in his "Covert Letter":

A Maryland physician was enjoying a free afternoon walking through the countryside. Coming upon an old farm house he walked into the front yard to ask whether he could get a drink from the well. As he knocked on the door a tiny little girl in pigtails, no more than eight years old, came to the screen door. "Nobody's here. They's gone to town to buy groceries."

Standing there, unimpressively dressed in khaki

pants, knit shirt and walking shoes, the doctor told the little girl that he just wanted to get a drink of cool water from the well. The little girl said, "The well is dry—it's never had any water in it. But I'll bring you a glass of cold milk, if you will just wait here on the porch!" He gladly accepted the glass of milk, and then another, thanked the child and was on his way.

A few months later, the emergency room of a Baltimore hospital came alive when a mother and father brought in a crying child. The doctor on duty explained that immediate attention was necessary, for the child was having an appendicitis attack. Despite the fact that there was no insurance and no money, the parents signed papers permitting the operation.

Several days passed, and the parents knew they would have to pay the bill. They were distraught with worry. Finally, en route to take their little daughter home, the parents stopped by the finance office of the hospital, fearful in wondering how they would arrange to carry the bill and secure her release. To their total astonishment, the bill was marked, "Paid in full by two glasses of milk," and signed by the doctor![7]

Parenting Provides Security

Parental trust combined with direction for a child is essential to incorporating values into the child's life. Such influence is especially important in the development of authentic self-understanding and a wholesome sexuality which are directly related to trust. A child learns from its parents to say with security, "I am female," "I am male." A wholesome sense of sexual identity is important at an early age in a child's development.

Children need to see the affection, the fidelity, and the

trust in their parents' relationship. They also need to feel the deep affirmation and acceptance of their own persons as sexual beings of unique personal worth. To be sexually affirmed without being violated is an essential contribution of family to personal development. More will be said about this later.

Relationship factors are also significant in a child's sexual development. Family means parent-child relationships of love and integrity. It includes admiration and affinity between children and parents, especially between sons and their mother, and between daughters and father. Here we develop the deep trust in which they can be affectionate without this being perverted into sexual violation.

An inability to trust a parent to relate in a wholesome manner can be extremely destructive in the child. It develops a fear of intimacy. Incest is a deep-seated problem in our society, and is evidence of a failure in respect and in the cultivation of trust in family relationships. (We will speak further on sexuality in chapter 5.)

Trust can not be demanded, nor can it be found by seeking it alone. Rather, trust is the spontaneous quality of faith-covenant in which each reaches out to the other, in affirmation of their worth and in encouragement of the very best in their personal and social life.

A child who cannot trust his/her parents becomes painfully insecure. Parental trust begins at birth as the baby trusts the mother for food and warmth.

We have seen so many inner-city children who don't know how to trust themselves to achieve in anything, because they can't trust their parent or parents for even such simple things as food and dry beds and rat-free sleep at night. They can't even trust the sexual behavior of their parents.

Esther taught art classes for some of these children for a couple of years. One child, we'll call her Pamela, was brought to her class by a worker in our church. She lived in a one-room apartment with her mother who was a prostitute. The mother didn't care enough for her to give her breakfast or send her to school, so our worker went to feed her and take her to school. When she came to class she sat at the table with the other children, but with her arms tightly wrapped across her chest and her head down. After several weeks of classes, and lots of love from Esther and the other workers, she finally reached out for crayons. For a while all that she drew were black circles that she colored purple inside. The art therapist explained that Pamela was trapped inside a painful situation. With continued love and encouragement there was a change, and after several months she entered right into all of the projects.

One day Esther went to get the children's small clay sculptures to put into the kiln for firing. Some lettering on the base of Pamela's sculpture of the bust of a girl caught her eye. As Esther looked more closely, she read the words, "The Lord Luvs Me Like I Am." As tears ran down her cheeks, she thanked God that Pamela had felt enough love and trust to recognize God's love, and that her securities were growing in this way.

Right priorities are essential for personal development, essential if we are to build a strong bond of trust. We need to be confident that the value of persons is above the valuing of things. Our way of life in the family ought to say, "You are much more important than all of the things that engage my life!"

Chapter Three
God's Sculpture Needs Intimacy and Fulfillment

Holy Father, protect them by the power of Your name—the name You gave Me—so that they may be one as We are One (John 17:11).

Sex we can do without, but intimacy we cannot. One of humanity's greatest needs is intimacy. We were created in and for relationship. We are incomplete until there is a meaningful relationship that calls us beyond ourselves into an intimacy that shares with but does not use another.

In Genesis 1, we read how God, the Sculptor, demonstrated the importance of intimacy when He created the first family. He stooped down beside a river and took into His hands a lump of clay. He intimately fashioned the clay into His own image and blew into it His breath of life—and Adam became a living soul! What a beautiful demonstration of intimacy. Then, He saw that Adam needed a companion by his side, someone whom he could love and with whom, in the exercise of sexual intimacy, he could make a complete family. So God didn't use clay this time, but he took a rib from the side of Adam—not his back but his side, and made Eve of the same substance as Adam. Here is the classic story of love and intimacy.

Jesus' intimacy with the Father is a model of the unity, the togetherness, of genuine love. For us to share intimately there must be an authentic sense of oneness, of togetherness (John 17:3-12). Intimacy is possible only when we dare to be fully known by another. Intimacy is experienced only by the vulnerability that opens oneself totally to another.

Such intimacy is much more holistic than the intimacy thought of in our society which is basically sexual in nature. It is a "belonging" that is to be enjoyed by single as well as married, a social belonging to others beyond oneself, a belonging which is by its very nature transforming.

A 1985 denominational study done by the Mennonite Church, *Human Sexuality in the Christian Life,* states,

> One of the sharpest contrasts between the Christian and the secular view of sexuality is seen in the understanding and affirmation of true intimacy. Secular society promotes the notion that intimacy is the same as genital interaction. . . . Sex we can live without; what we cannot live without is intimacy. That is the real need of both men and women. . . .
>
> Unless love, trust, commitment, and the emotional and spiritual dimensions of true intimacy are present, physical sex is, at best, empty, and, at worst, distances the partners.[1]

Intimacy Is the Freedom of Covenant

Love grows by sharing our lives with each other. There is no substitute for time together, for communication, for participation together in the meanings of covenant. At the most practical level, love makes us partners in all of life. But unless we, by deliberate effort, make time together, it won't happen.

Special friends of ours, Bill and Dee Brehm of Washington D.C., are great examples for us in making time for intimacy. They are about our age, and ever since their marriage, they designated Wednesday evenings as *theirs.* Nothing could interrupt that night, barring illness or some special emergency. Dee prepares a special candlelight meal and gets dressed up in something beautiful. Bill comes in from his office and puts his briefcase inside the coat closet at the front door as a symbol that there will be no work that evening. They spend the evening at a leisurely dinner, talk, sing, or play a game. They won't talk about finances or work or difficulties—this is understood. Even after the children came to be part of the family, Wednesday evening was their night. The children were fed early and put to bed. As they grew older, Bill and Dee would take their candlelight dinner upstairs to their bedroom. The children knew it was Mom and Dad's night. What a model of intimate sharing for their children!

We all can't do it exactly that way. But each of us can schedule in specific times and places where we can spend time together alone as a couple.

Gibson Winter has written of our society:

> We are "in love with love," but we know too little about the full scope of love. We have yet to arrive at a real appreciation of responsible love which finds its fulfillment in life for one another. Many families possess the genuine article but vainly strive to recover the romance from which it emerged.[2]

The individualism of our Western world, the mechanization of life, and now the professionalization of life for both husband and wife—each works against meaningful intimacy. Intimacy means time together in the closeness of love and communication, for intimacy must grow. It is by sharing in thought, in worship, in dreams, and in a sense of purpose that the intimacy of spirit develops.

One of our severe social problems is that of teens seeking an intimacy which includes being sexually active, without an understanding of the need for holistic intimacy. This accounts for the thousands of births annually by unwed teenage mothers. It also explains why abortion is so easy for many persons who regard the fetus as an "it" rather than as a "person"; they find the presence of a new life a hindrance rather than a new facet of the joy of intimacy. For many, sex becomes a substitute for the deeper meaning of intimacy which they are seeking, an escape from the disciplines of spirit that enable persons to relate unselfishly.

Family is the place in which the larger meaning of intimacy should be experienced. Families can experience an intimacy that will help children to avoid ever thinking they can be satisfied with sexual engagement without the full meaning of love. Life is too large, too great, and too profound to be fulfilled by indulging only one facet of sharing. And our relationship with each other is too important, too meaningful, and too rewarding to be engaged in other than in a mutually enriching partnership.

In the actual experiences of life we pursue what we value. This is more than simply acknowledging in our minds that some things are good or important. It is a matter of "valuing" them as important and consequently pursuing them as a part of our lifestyle. Often we believe something to be good, like physical exercise, but we don't value it enough to go through the discipline of doing it. Intimacy is a value of spirit, of the inner self. Intimacy is an expression of love; it is "to prize someone and to be prized. It is to choose and to be chosen, to be needed and important to another."[3] Intimacy is the ability to transcend self-interests in a genuine act of sharing with the other.

> Intimacy is selfless,
> openness to another,
> sharing without demand,
> engaging social enrichment,
> belonging in equity,
> loving in mutuality.
> Intimacy is emotive covenant.

Gibson Winter claims that the average American is incapable of a really intimate relationship because he/she is too selfish. But he offers hope for us.

If we mean by intimacy the relationship in which people know one another, support one another, share their lives, and identify their interests with one another, then the modern family can be an extremely intimate group . . . while modern life has intensified our need for intimate relationships, it has also weakened our capacity to sustain an intimate relationship.[4]

Gibson sees modernity as resulting in the shrinking of both men and women, resulting in a shrinking of the self. Christian grace has the transforming power to change this, and instead of shrinking, we will find the abundant life!

Intimacy is the truly personal aspect of love, for love is opening one's life deeply to the person and life of another.

Intimacy includes another fully,
shares with one another honestly,
relates in a way that is truly open,
and enjoys the bonding of oneness.

In intimacy there are no hidden areas that are deliberately closed to the other. This is essential to a happy marriage and to an enriching family experience.

To be intimate is basically to think with the other, to be fully sensitive to the other, to share love in respect for the mutual worth and joy of each.

Intimacy never uses the other,
never violates the spirit or life of the other,
never manipulates or coerces the other,
never closes the other out of your life.

Sexuality defines our way of living as persons. But sexual drives are not all that sexuality is about, and the satisfaction of these drives is not the chief good. What is lacking in our society is intimacy of spirit. As we wrestle with both the minute pressures and the megatrends of our day, we tend to put a person into categories as an "it." This keeps us from looking the other in the eye and seeing one who is equally created in the image of God.

One writer has said, "High tech calls for high touch." We must emphasize again the statement, "Sex we can live without, but what we cannot live without is intimacy!" Each of us has the need for warm, close, intimate contact, and this is a need that continues throughout life. This intimacy is not basically a need for sexual intercourse, but is rather the need for tenderness, gentleness, esteem, and a love that affirms one's highest worth.

Intimacy grows as we are willing to be vulnerable, to run the risks of "being known." Intimacy means that we "tune in" to each other, that we take time to hear one another, to share in honesty and trust. Intimacy is the evidence that we care about one another, about how the other feels. The development of an intimate understanding relationship will respect the needs of the other and will avoid making demands. This will include respecting times in which the other may need to be alone.

To be alone gives one the space to think things through without distractions; it gives space for creative thoughts; it separates one from the mundane routine to make room for the imagination and a new focus. The experience of being alone occasionally can bring to the marriage new energy, new focus, new excitement and eagerness. Lois Wyse expresses this factor in relation to her own marriage:

> There is within each of us
>   A private place
>   For thinking private thoughts
>   And dreaming private dreams.
>
> But in the shared experience of marriage,
> Some people cannot stand the private partner.

How fortunate for me
That you have let me grow,
Think my private thoughts,
Dream my private dreams.

And bring a private me
To the shared experience of marriage.[5]

Open Ourselves to God

If a couple has not learned to share, they make a mistake in not facing this as their major problem. It is never good to substitute sex for intimacy. Having sex is a poor way to get to really know a person. But when properly related to the larger meaning of intimacy, then the deepest meaning of sex in the scriptural statement is fulfilled, "The two shall become one flesh" (Ephesians 5:31).

Intimacy is a support base for the human personality. It is in close relationships that we experience acceptance, understanding, encouragement, and reciprocal caring. Such intimacy is most fully shared when it is also shared with God; in fact it is in laying one's life intimately open to Him, in surrender and identity, that we learn to be intimate with one another. In his book, *The Mystery of Marriage*, Mike Mason says:

> Not that anything like a perfect society will ever be possible in this world — but still there is an instinctual sense that marriage leads the way, that universal peace can only be conceived of in terms of human beings coming together with something of the same spirit of love, unity, commitment, and self-sacrifice that are seen to operate at the heart of a good marriage. Marriage is the test case, the leading edge, and the sine qua non of love and brotherhood in the world. For all these reasons, good marriages are the foundation of society.[6]

The intimacy that we, Myron and Esther, have found and enjoy in our personal relationship is one that has grown, especially as we have matured in our faith experiences. As a result we are more intimate in our love and at the same time more free in our respect for each other and much less inclined to be controlling. We enjoy life more, enjoy each other more, and see more of the humor in life rather than focusing so much on details. We are more free in our prayers and in our conversations about Jesus and His will for us. M. Scott Peck writes:

> I have come to believe and have tried to demonstrate that (any) people's capacity to love, and hence their will to grow, is nurtured not only by their parents during childhood, but also through out their lives by grace, or God's love.[7]

It was our privilege to know Corrie Ten Boom, the wonderful Dutch woman of *The Hiding Place.* Myron enjoys the memories of sharing the platform and of having lunch with her in Lausanne, Switzerland. She had her own particular sense of humor. For example, in her forthright but intimate style, discussing eschatology, she told us of a trip to America when she asked Dr. J. Edwin Orr about the views in the American churches on our Lord's second coming, as divided into "a -, pre -, and post-millennial" interpretations. She laughed as she quoted his jest in answer to her question. "My dear Corrie," he said, "that is a-pre-post-erous question!"

But her intimacy with God is what most impressed us. Corrie was close to God in a most personal way, learned and shared through many suffering experiences. Her mentoring of this intimacy is expressed in a story told by Leighton Ford, involving his daughter.

During a conference which Leighton and Corrie shared as speakers, he had taken his daughter Debbie to visit Corrie at the home where she was staying. At the close of their conversation, Corrie said very simply, "Let's talk to the Father." With no change of voice or posture she simply closed her eyes and began talking to God as naturally as she had been talking to them.

As they drove toward home, Debbie was quiet, and then she said to Leighton, "Dad, I had the most weird feeling while Corrie was praying; I almost think I had a vision. There was a long hall and Corrie was walking down it. At the end were these large doors with a sliver of light showing underneath. As she got to the doors, some guards swung the doors open and welcomed her with a smile. Past the doors there was this large brilliantly lighted room with a throne in the center. I could see Corrie walk up to God's throne. And as she approached, I imagined God saying, "Well, hello, Corrie. What can I do for you today?"

This is the characteristic of a mature faith which leads to intimacy with God. When we open our lives at their very heart to a personal, intimate relationship with God, we have transcended the selfish rebellion that has isolated us from Him. With this victory in grace we are then enabled to open our lives to others. This is one dynamic of prayer. Intimate prayer will be for the family not simply an expression of piety, but the practice of opening our lives together to the one Lord who ministers alike to each of us.

This principle also applies horizontally to our social relationships. The spirit of openness, of willingness to include others, to share intimacy with them, calls us to reach beyond ourselves. Ralph Waldo Emerson said, "The only way to have a friend is to be one." Family is the primary unit in which we teach and extend social values. Children are enriched by a home in which visitors are welcomed, in which the parents are actively engaged in hosting, and in which the children listening in on conversations discern things of importance to their parents and their peers.

Principles of social justice, of caring for the poor, of reaching beyond our ethnic group or family of origin to include persons of other groups and races in our circles of fellowship and social influence, are to be modeled in the home. If we are to prepare our young people to live in a pluralistic society with selectivity, to relate to others as a Christian presence without compromise, to be able to love and share with persons different from themselves, and to take their place as responsible participants in the global community, we need to model this in the patterns of our home and family life.

Children catch the spirit of care for the suffering from their parents. When our daughter Marcia was ten years old, we were preparing for a family trip to India. We planned to be gone two months. After we discussed our problem of what we do with her dearly loved poodle dog, Pepper, she initiated the plan to sell her. It was a hard decision, but we put an ad in the paper. When Marcia saw the ad, she burst into tears with regret. So when the calls began to come from potential buyers, Esther simply said, "Our daughter is heartbroken and has changed her mind; the dog is no longer for sale."

After several days, Marcia answered the phone. It was a lady who asked about the dog. Esther heard Marcia try to explain the change of plans. As she came away from the phone she was smiling with joy. "The lady is coming for my dog tomorrow!" "Oh?" Esther inquired with surprise. "Yes," replied Marcia. "She has a foster home with several children who are begging for a dog. She offered to keep Pepper while we're gone!" That was great news for us all, except we were uneasy about Pepper's unpredictable disposition at times. Once in a while she would snap at someone. So when the lady arrived we told her about this, but she still wanted to take Pepper.

On the way home two months later, on our last flight of the trip, Marcia was unusually quiet. After a couple hours of this Esther asked, "Marcia, you are so quiet. Do you want to talk about what is on your mind?" She had thought it all through, "Mom, I can't take Pepper away from those children. They don't even have a normal family; they need her worse than I do. I'm going to let them keep her." With that she buried her face in Esther's lap and cried a little while, then lifted her head like a little soldier. "Mom, I've made the right decision." We were pretty proud parents. Young children seem to sense the needs of other children very quickly. This gift needs to be nurtured in the family so that it is carried into adulthood. Children are not concerned about racial and cultural differences. They become prejudiced only when they see it modeled in adults.

Christians should engage the mission of being a presence for Christ in the world. The family should become the basis for this mission, fulfilling what Paul called "the church in thy house" (Philemon 2). We believe that a conservative theology does not necessarily call for a conservative social or political view. A conservative mentality wed to a parochial Americanism will make us selfish and exclusive, when we should be taking our place as Christian neighbors in the global community.

Each Christian family is a unit of the kingdom of Christ, where the evidence of living by God's rule is to be seen. We model together what it means to profess Jesus as Lord and to live as His servants. There is no greater purpose, no higher calling, than to serve Christ in serving others.

Among Esther's sculptures are two very expressive works, one quite realistic and the other semi-abstract on the same theme, of Jesus washing Peter's feet. The semi-abstract work was built by Esther on the campus of Union Biblical Seminary, Pune, India, as a statement of their motto from Ephesians 4:15, "Truthing in love." It is a statement of a Christ-centered lifestyle, serving rather than controlling others. Jesus said, "Do to others as you would have them do to you" (Luke 6:31).

Chapter Four
God's Sculpture Expresses Sexuality and Wholeness

Then the Lord God made a woman from the rib He had taken out of the man, and He brought her to the man. The man said, "This is now bone of my bones and flesh of my flesh; she shall be called woman, for she was taken out of man." For this reason a man will leave his father and mother and be united to his wife, and they will become one flesh. The man and his wife were both naked and they felt no shame (Genesis 2:22-25).

God created us in His image, "male and female He created them" (Genesis 1:27). Sexuality is an essential aspect of our identity. Each of us is a sexual being, he or she, created alike in the image of God. Sexuality is the *nature* of our being; genital sex is the *appetite* that accompanies being a sexual person.

A sculptor fashioning a piece of sculpture works with many shapes or parts in creating a whole, a unity so that the many parts blend into one. If one of these parts "sticks out" or is given more strength than the rest, the sculptor works to reduce that strength, or to balance the visual whole by strengthening another part. Esther recalls being told in art school that one part looked "tacked on," or another part of the sculpture was weak. Each part must become one with the whole for there to be equal balance.

So it is in family. We have many individual parts which have their own unique value, but if one overpowers the others, a wholeness of the family sculpture cannot be achieved.

God sculpts man and woman with equal but respective visual beauty, equal capacities and abilities, as male and female bring balance and wholeness to the family. When God sculpts the family, He places husband and wife in a relationship of loving respect, with the children, in openness and harmony with each other as a statement of the intrinsic worth of each individual. This relationship gives sexuality its glory.

Sex is a gift of God. At the highest level of God's intentions, it could be thought of as a marriage sacrament. In the marriage covenant there is a sacredness of transcending oneself in the mutual pleasure of passionate belonging! In the relationship of a man and woman in covenant for life, there is a sense of worship and wonder in the mutuality of the sexual experience.

This stands in stark contrast to the selfish level to which sex has been reduced in our general society. The argument is that if there is mutual hunger and consent, and if no one is hurt, it is acceptable. For persons holding this view, sex is coupled with the self-centered use of another, rather than with true self-fulfillment with and for another. This selfish mind-set has exploited sex through entertainment and advertisement. And with the plague of AIDS accompanying social promiscuity, the talk is of "safe sex," or now of "safer sex," rather than of waiting until marriage and of fidelity in marriage. We lack an adequate understanding of personhood and of sexuality.

Each of us, being made in the image of God, has the power to think, to love, to fellowship, to make decisions, to be morally responsible, to be creative, to be unique in our persons. A part of this uniqueness is sexuality, that which makes us male or female. And since each alike is created in the image of God, it is in maleness and femaleness together that we have the more complete expression of the imago Dei. Dietrich Bon-hoeffer wrote:

> They were one from their origin and only when they become one do they return to their origin. This

becoming one is never the fusion of the two, the abolition of their creatureliness as individuals. It is the utmost possible realization of their belonging to one another, which is based directly upon the fact that they are different from one another. . . .

In the context of the whole it can only be that woman becomes man's helper in the carrying of the limit imposed upon him. . . . Free life can only be borne in limitation if it is loved, and out of this mercy He created a companion for man who must be at once the embodiment of Adam's limit and the object of his love.[1]

The two becoming one, finding the unity of the imago Dei in this relationship, means that it is in this very oneness that sexuality achieves its wholeness, in the freedom and in the limits with which God has endowed us. But sexuality is not to be reduced to mean merely sex. When society speaks of the sexual, it too often means genital sex and thus misses the larger meaning of wholeness.

A husband and wife enjoy their sexuality together, and are proud of each other as they fulfill their roles as sexual beings. As parents, we model for our children an identity and joy in being male and female. Wholesome development of male and female identity is derived from a genuine respect for the sexual identity of each member of the family. When this is lacking, young adults may be driven for years by the unfulfilled quest of answering the questions of the essential nature of their personal identities as sexual beings.

Mutual Submission Is a Special Grace

Colleen Evans, a close friend to Esther, writes:

Sexual unity calls for the ultimate in mutual submission, as two people present themselves to each other, accepting each other just as they are. It is a

> test of trust, one that, in the beginning, requires
> courage for total unmasking of body and soul. For
> oneness means giving up the very personal and pri-
> vate you. This kind of submission is not easy. For
> some it is much harder than for others; yet it is well
> worth the abandonment of self which it requires.
> Unless two people can both surrender to the other,
> and also both be willing to be initiators, they will
> miss some of the specialness and oneness God has
> created for them.[2]

Human nature tends to separate sex from the larger meaning of sexuality and from the wholeness of life. We have isolated sex as a hunger from its meaning as a gift from God. As a consequence we have an emphasis on passion without purity, on recreational sex without meaningful relationship, and on cohabitation without covenant.

As we write these lines, the news in Washington, D.C. is filled with cases of rape, violence, incest, and child abuse. Sexual harassment is now a frequent charge, with accounts of how one person violates another in words or actions. It is appalling to find teenagers shooting other teenagers out of jealousy over a girl, with little sense of remorse!

We need to rediscover what Merton and Irene Strommen call "intrinsic values," respect for the personal dignity and freedom of individuals, respect for the basic human ties of family, respect for the physical and psychological health of people, and respect for the rights of individuals. Parallel with these intrinsic values they also list moral values: fidelity—keeping promises, honesty—being truthful, sexual restraint—control of sexual appetite, and social justice—protecting the powerless.[3]

Sexuality Creates Worth

The elders of our congregation in Washington, D.C. (where we served as founders of the church in 1981, as pastoral team members, and in which Myron presently serves as a minister of the Word), developed a statement in 1990 as an interpretation of discipleship in our relationships as sexual beings. The statement, affirming the worth of each person in the mutual experience of God's grace, and intended to stimulate dialogue, has nine points:

1. We accept fully the biblical truth that male and female are alike created in the image of God, and that masculinity and femininity together express the fuller meaning of the image of God.

2. We believe that disciples of Jesus Christ will recognize the people of God as expressed in the congregation as the primary community for relationship beyond the immediate family unit. We emphasize the importance of masculine and feminine relationships as a fellowship in which single and married share together in social enrichments that benefit from our sexuality without sex.

3. We affirm the biblical teaching of God's plan for marriage being a one man/one woman relation for life, in a relationship of mutual submission, complementary rather than competitive. God may lead some persons to singleness and others to marriage. We believe that divorce is a sin. Forgiveness is possible through repentance, and God will help persons to build again, sometimes including a new marriage.

4. We see God's emphasis in Scripture to be on the family as the basic social unit, and on husband and wife relationships as the one basis for sexual intercourse.

5. We believe that premarital or extramarital sexual relations are wrong and are a perversion of the union which God creates.

6. We hold that same-sex orientation is not a created gift from God, but is a consequence of the brokenness of creation as a result of the fall of humanity, with which we must deal by the strength of divine grace.

7. We are committed to helping both unmarried hetero-

sexuals and same-sex oriented persons to live chaste and celibate lives.

8. We believe, as Dietrich Bonhoeffer has stated, "The essence of chastity is not the suppression of lust, but the total orientation of one's life towards a goal," pursuing Christ. Healthy chastity can be supported only by loving, positive involvement with members of the opposite sex. Alienation from them makes room for harmful lusts.

9. We will seek to avoid legalistic judgments that reject persons who struggle with understanding and/or expressing their sexuality, and will seek to share loving acceptance while holding such persons accountable for holiness in their lives.

This statement is an attempt not only to guide but to free persons for meaningful social intimacy in the congregation. It seeks to incorporate single with married in a common community of love and social enrichment. It is our attempt at a biblical theology of sexuality. It results from our study of many passages, especially the Creation accounts and related New Testament interpretations of them.

Sex Can Be "Sacrament"

The other person is the limit placed upon me by God. I love this limit and I shall not transgress it because of my love. This means nothing except that the two, who remain two as creatures of God, become one body, i.e. belong to one another in love. In the creation of the other person, freedom and creatureliness are bound together in love. That is why the other person is grace to the first, just as the prohibition to eat of the tree of knowledge was grace. In this common bearing of the limit, by the first two human beings in community, is tested the character of this community as the Church.[4]

Fulfillment of sexuality calls for the disciplines of one's sexual nature for the wholeness of life. When any part of one's personality gets out of balance, and seeks to rule the whole, life itself is warped. Thomas More, in Robert Bolt's play, *A Man for All Seasons,* speaks of "that little area in which I must rule myself." Each of us has such an area, and we need the power of the Spirit to be master and not be mastered.

When love toward the other is destroyed, one will only hate his limit; married couples will then lose the deepest treasures of joy in each other in their experience of sex. We need to be reminded that sex is not just something we do; it is something we are together. We are one in being one.

> Sexuality is to be celebrated.
>> It is me, who I am,
>> male or female,
>> created in God's image,
>> my identity as a person,
>> the enjoyment of being me.
> Sexuality calls me to worship the Creator.

To help set the above in the context of our larger social relationships, we offer the following premises:

1. We need to see marriage as a matter of community. It is not a private matter alone, for it is a call to express covenant with integrity while sharing socially with others, single and married in the community of faith.

2. We need to see singleness as one means of developing a secure personality. Singleness should be accepted and enjoyed before one enters a covenant of marriage. This will enable one to bring to friendships and love a complementary rather than a controlling relationship.

3. We need to see singleness as an opportunity to develop as unitary beings, with the harmony of an integrated self, so that one's life is not mastered by sex, but rather that one

is able to channel sexual energy into other than physical release.

4. We need to find in celibacy a choice to orient life in the service of Christ and His kingdom without the mitigating responsibilities of even wholesome obligations to another.

5. We need sexual integrity as an order of life that will free us in community for meaningful social relations, without our motives being misconstrued.

Integrity Is Essential for Community

We need to ask some questions of congregations that seek to provide a meaningful community in which singles and married are ministered to equally. The community of faith should be an interpreting community in which we help each other raise questions, and then find and follow the will of God.

1. How does our experience with our past—for example, fear of authority or fear of being violated—keep us from the openness of intimacy?

2. How can the Christian community promote spiritual and psychological intimacy without sexuality being turned to sex itself?

3. How can the community support singles in sharing aspects of life which will enhance intimacy? Conversely, how can singles share with married couples in enriching forms of friendship?

4. How can we help each other, married or single, to engage a holy intimacy that transcends our western individualism?

5. How can we develop meaningful intimate friendships with persons of the same sex without this being a sexual fixation?

6. How can we differentiate between being "in love with love" and being able to love the person?

7. How can we develop more whole-person communica-

tion with the trust and respect that enables disciplined intimacy?

Life is complex, for human relations are complex. We find this especially evident in Paul's treatment in 1 Corinthians 7 and Ephesians 5. Clearly the married couple needs a third ground between them, a ground of spiritual principles, for this will provide security as they relate in family life. Authentic community—to borrow an idea from Bonhoeffer *(Life Together)*—means that two persons relate to each other in and through Christ. By relating in and through Christ, each one is free and yet in covenant. Such freedom provides the security that we will not be manipulated, coerced, controlled, intimidated, or violated by the other person. In this freedom each can bring to the other the intimacy of spiritual covenant, and the undergirding of trust.

Sex Education Is Essential

Good sex education is an essential for the development of children, and as preparation for their future relationships. It is important that much of this be done early in their learning experience, preferably before puberty, before physiological developments and emotional embarrassments keep them from hearing objectively.

Too often parents are hesitant to talk about sex with their children, even though their lifestyle in the family is already giving the child insights to their relationship. Some parents are afraid to let others teach their children about sex. Good schools and church youth leaders can model trust and community in sharing together to seek the best understanding and disciplines for our children.

On the front page of the *Washington Post,* December 23, 1991, was an article by Laura Sessions Stepp, entitled, "Being Blunt about the Birds and Bees." The subtitle was, "In AIDS Era, Parents Are More to the Point with Children in

Discussing Sex." In the article Stepp analyzes interviews with twenty middle-class parents in the Washington, D.C. area. These indicate that with AIDS and the high rate of teenage pregnancy, there is much more discussion by parents with their children about sex. Quoting Mary Pappas, who has run sex-education workshops in the area for ten years, she emphasizes that parents "are eager now to be involved with their children's sex education." As Christian parents, we cannot fail our families on this important issue; we need to talk with them and not just to them.

One of Myron's esteemed colleagues in the Christian College Coalition staff, Steve Garber, of the American Studies Program, often shares his reflections in notes to us as colleagues. He and his wife, Meg, are dedicated parents of five wonderful children. They take seriously the issue of sex education in a Christian context. In December of 1991, Steve wrote:

> But as I listen to my culture, it is the phrase "safe sex" that is most troubling. What does it mean for those of us who want to nurture in our children a moral imagination which understands the meaning of God's good gift of sexuality?
>
> As the editorialists and commentators tell us, we can use condoms and ask questions . . . and that is safe sex. How is it safe? It protects us from the risk of sexually transmitted diseases. Since these diseases — AIDS in particular — are "everybody's problem," no one of us is immune. We are all at risk, or so we are told. . . . It is as if no serious person could dare question the inevitability of sexual infidelity, and as if no serious person would ever ask more of sex than safety.
>
> But we do, don't we? Not only do we as the people of Christ, thinking and living as the salt and light of society, and therefore questioning the assumptions which so shape our common good. But we do as human beings too.[5]

Steve is right. Perversion in sexual behavior is a social issue of magnitude, and because Christians are not immune from this phenomena of society, we are in this together. We need to find nonjudgmental approaches by which we can share Christian values. The late G. Arthur Keough reminded us, "Greatness is not standing above our fellows and ordering them around; it is standing with them and helping them to be all they can be." This is the pattern of servanthood. But the difficult thing about a theology of servanthood is *being* a servant. John Stott has written in commentary on the biblical metaphors of salt and light that it is senseless to blame the meat for spoiling! It is senseless to curse the room for its darkness! The question is always, "Where was the salt? Where is the light?"

Our model for wholeness in sexuality is Jesus Himself, the One who gave Himself totally for us. In His person He brought together the best values of life from the masculine and the feminine aspects of personhood. He was a very masculine person in His dedication, forthrightness, boldness, decisiveness, care for others, work habits, etc. He also incorporated those characteristics so prominent in the feminine person, for while He was loving, strong, and had leadership qualities, He was also compassionate, gentle, emotionally intuitive, and was able to engage persons with understanding.

Jesus brought the two together in His keen feeling of the worth of persons, His deep feeling for relationships, and His close touch with the source of life. But He challenged the very perversions that beset us: competition, success, power, prestige, status, wealth, property, fighting, proving oneself in struggles for dominance. Jesus enjoyed relating to men and women; for example, He had women in His company of disciples (Luke 8:1-3), and He enjoyed spending time with Martha and Mary (Luke 10:38-42). It is proper to say that Jesus enjoyed sexuality without needing sex. He enjoyed the richness of relationships of integrity. His times in the home of Martha and Mary are expressions of His enjoyment of social relationships. By His patterns He calls us to a freedom which enjoys but doesn't violate intimacy.

Our first parents in the Garden of Eden were created innocent but immature. Maturity comes by making decisions that enable us to grow. Adam and Eve made decisions, but in a very basic one they blew it! They were created for community, to walk intimately together and to make basic decisions together. The story tells us that as Eve listened to the Serpent, her man was there with her! (Genesis 3:6) They were in this together. But she violated their community and usurped personal authority by initiating a decision on something which had implications for both of them (1 Timothy 2:12-14).

Concerning Adam's involvement with Eve, the Prophet Hosea said years later of Israel, "Like Adam, they have broken the covenant—they were unfaithful to Me there" (Hosea 6:7). The intimacy between them should not only have involved them in mutual decision-making, but should have continued to include their being intimate with God. Without faithfulness to this primary relation with God, they broke covenant, suffering the death of the most important reality of the spirit, intimacy with God.

Relationships of wholesome intimacy and full community are the evidence that we are participating in God's transforming grace. In this new creation we recognize that our intimacy includes our sharing with Him, as often expressed by Paul's phrase, "in Christ." In turn, we can love and enjoy persons without using them. We can actually meet God in one another as we share together in Christ.

Wholeness means completeness. This can not be known without seeing ourselves as whole. We are unitary beings, not personalities that can be cut into parts, to engage or even to indulge one part without holding it in full relationship with the totality of person. This oneness, this being unitary beings, helps us to understand what it means to become "one flesh" with another.

In the relationship of authentic covenant sexual experience the two become one, become a whole together, refusing to separate any one function of life from the whole of relationship. To use the biblical word, this is to truly "know" one's companion. This is the wholeness of marriage covenant, the deepest spirit of community.

Chapter Five
God's Sculpture Is Bonded by Faith

Speaking the truth in love, we will in all things grow up into Him who is the Head, that is, Christ. From Him the whole body, joined and held together by every supporting ligament, grows and builds itself up in love, as each part does its work (Ephesians 4:15-16).

In making a sculpture Esther sometimes uses bronze in powder form. The powdered bronze needs a bonding material to turn it into a strong, solid mass. So she mixes two liquids, epoxy, and a catalyst. The catalyst is the key to the strength of the sculpture. The bronze powder, which can be brushed or blown away, and the liquid epoxy, which is like water, will never harden by themselves. When the catalyst is present, they are bonded together into an almost unbreakable mass or form.

Faith is the catalyst which bonds the individual parts of a marriage or family. Without faith there can be no bonding.

Bonding means to form lasting, intimate, faithful relationships. It is one of the greater qualities of humanness. This is especially powerful in the Christian family, where the presence of Christ through the Holy Spirit provides a common bonding of mutual faith. This faith is an essential ingredient for meaningful relationships, for it becomes the common foundation for each family member and the ground on which trust is exercised.

A family sculptured by God will be a community of faith. Each person will share in a circle that is not broken and that expresses the bonding of faith and love. The expression of this circle will change as individual family members mature and seek their own roles or fulfillment, but the bonding of faith and love will remain their strength.

Merton and Irene Strommen write:

> We believe that each source of strength within the family contributes to the growth and development of an adolescent. We also believe that a liberating religious faith enhances each characteristic. We use the word "liberating" faith because our studies evidence two types: a forgiveness-oriented faith and a guilt-oriented faith. One is freeing and the other enslaving.[1]

Even when the teenage adolescent seeks autonomy by distancing, an action that frequently includes distancing from the faith of the family for a time, it is often this liberating faith-bonding that brings the young person back to the faith of the family. While it is not a determinism, this liberating faith which allows them to distance includes a recognition and respect for the development of a young person's life, so that what they come to believe becomes their own firsthand faith rather than a borrowed creed.

As Christians we will live in the circle of meaning that makes of our family a special unit. This bonding of faith means that we live in relation to the risen Christ. As we recognize His presence among us, our relation to each other takes on a different character. We stand with each other, not over against one another. We are there when one stumbles to help him or her rise again, and we are there to celebrate the successes of each one in the mutual joy of commonality.

Maturing Means Growing Together

None of us are perfect; therefore, the positive influence of the home is not a claim that parents do everything right. Rather, the parents' spirit, the honesty, and their own turning to the deeper meanings of faith impact the growing child. No parents come from perfect homes. Each of us is shaped by what we do with our experiences, by our own processing of both complementary and confusing incidents of the past.

Sigmund Freud has shown how the effects of traumatic childhood experiences may carry over into our adult lives. We parents need to demonstrate in a positive light that we also deal with hurtful memories of past experiences that could still affect us. This faith-realism will communicate an honesty about the dynamic of faith. In turn this will help each child to deal with things that we as parents can't erase or control, happenings that are life experiences.

Because faith is not coerced, parents need to understand the nature of faith development. We have no guarantee that a child will come to meaningful faith. We seek to model the faith, but each person is responsible for the synthesis of thought and the decisions that shape life. But a wholesome influence is a special dynamic in helping a growing child to arrive at an informed and growing faith.

In the Anabaptist/Mennonite tradition of believer's baptism, or adult confession of faith, preparation and respect for voluntary choice at a responsible age is an important part of the life of the church. In fact, it is a special aspect of our life in community and our concern, lest children be pushed by peer pressure to ask for baptism at a premature age. We want them to make step-by-step commitments to Jesus in their faith development as growing children. This should then be confirmed as a public witness in baptism at a more mature age when the meaning of conversion from being self-oriented to being Christ-oriented is understood.

Growing together in our experiences of faith provides a

common and authentic bonding of oneness. The congregation is responsible to surround both parents and children with loving encouragement to be fully involved in the life of faith in the community. This begins with the child's birth, the dedication of the infant in public worship, and the involvement of the child in the very best in nurture. But this also includes the parents in a meaningful fellowship, as other members take responsibility for being to one another loving participants in the grace of God. As Mother Teresa has said, "Man's greatest sin is not hatred, but indifference to one's brothers and sisters," and this applies not only to the poor but to all persons, including the "covenant children" of a congregation.

The majority of our congregation here in Washington is young families. When babies are dedicated, the children of the congregation are invited to come to the front and support the baby with their presence. This is a symbol of their importance in the family of faith as well as of the new baby's place in this family circle. It helps the children to feel an ownership in the family. As children grow older, they may question the faith, but this bonding helps them to ask legitimate questions in the context of the community of faith.

At times we have listened to some of the deepest heart cries of young adults, questions that are as old as history but as real as today, as they ask where God is in the midst of adversity. Some questions imply that if God is around and active, certain situations should not exist. Other questions imply that the disciplines of daily life for the sake of a coming benefit are too much like pie-in-the-sky. We try to show them that the daily pattern of training by the athlete before the one glorious exhibition in which the crown is won is simply the realism of achievement. So it is with the disciplines of life.

In his teaching and preaching, Myron has tried to clarify that God does not overcome evil by a quick act of His superior power, but by the victory of His holiness and goodness. This approach means that the victory over evil comes by exposing evil in total contrast with the superior quality of goodness, an exposé that witnesses to the wonderful quality of righteousness in contrast to unrighteousness. And this exposé is worked out in actual life situations.

As parents listening to the questions of "Why?" we have to be honest about our own questions. We may have sought to walk with Christ as consistently as we know how, to serve Him as genuinely as we are able, to give ourselves to His church and His kingdom; and yet when difficult things happen, we have to wrestle with the question, "Why has this happened?"

Even so, we will turn again and again to the grace of God for the ability to accept what we can't change, and to be gracious in forgiveness and acceptance. We each learn through problems that help us to grow, and we then sort out the things that are eternally important.

As we have matured as a family we have learned to share with one another at new and deeper levels of thought, not all at the same time, but by thinking and discovering together how to bring life under the lordship of Christ. Family is one place that we should never lose the meaning of this quest.

In the family we should engage one another in the deeper levels of mutual faith (Colossians 3:17-21). As Christ has dealt with us in grace, so we are to deal with one another. This is first of all an affirmation of love. In the spirit of love, we can extend grace as a personal interest in the other. Our genuine support becomes the positive discipline that holds the other accountable for the best in the discipleship of Christ.

Forgiving One Another Is the Price of Love

Because we are sinful, and a long way from perfect, the only way we can have joyful, free relationships is if we forgive one another our wrongs. This is one of the central aspects of the Christian faith, and is also central to human relations.

Our need to forgive each other daily is a constant reminder of our faith-relation with God. Our social need to be forgiven by each other reminds us of our need to be forgiven by God. This need is inescapable, because of our very real imperfections, and our need for renewal of relationships.

The refusal to forgive is actually a power play. Refusing another the release of forgiveness is to keep the other person under your thumb, to make them squirm, to hold something over them that you can use to intimidate or manipulate. Unforgiveness is the ultimate expression of selfishness that seeks to dominate another in spirit as well as in life.

Forgiveness is always in relationship, and it expects the restoration of relationship. But forgiveness is unconditional! We dare not say, "I'll forgive if . . . " There is a difficult but necessary distinction between *expecting* a change through forgiveness and the domineering attitude of *requiring* a change!

To forgive is to release another. It is to acknowledge that the other person is more important than the issue. Myron has commented in preaching on this theme that in those times when he and Esther were "having words," he should have had the grace to just put his arm around her and close the distance by saying, "Honey, it doesn't matter; all that matters is you, and our love." But self-interests being what they are, we add words to words to prove a point. In doing so, we may win the battle but lose the war!

We have often been challenged by a demonstration of forgiveness from Myron's father. Clarence was foreman on a building job, constructing apartment buildings in Newport News, Virginia, near the shipyards. As a Christian he lived out his faith in relationship to some difficult employees, several of whom would have liked to have his position. One of them, Bob, created some tensions that gave Dad a very serious problem. Some time later a large number of men were laid off work, and Bob was among them. Myron remembers his dad telling the family that evening how painful it was for him to walk through the gate and see these men outside wishing for work and employment. One day he created several jobs and went up to the gate to choose some men. Many of them pushed to the fore, wanting him to hire them, but Bob stayed to the back, too embarrassed to come forward. Clarence called some, looking at Bob several times and then turning to another; but then he turned back to Bob, his enemy, and said, "Bob, get your tools and come along."

About fifteen years later, Myron was in Newport News in an evangelistic preaching mission. On the first Sunday evening, when he gave the invitation for persons to respond in commitment to Christ, among those who came was an older man. Myron stepped down to shake hands with him, and the man asked, "Do you know Clarence Augsburger?" Myron said, "He is my dad." The man was in tears as he replied, "He is why I am here." This former colleague on the job had been convicted through Clarence's demonstration of a forgiving spirit.

Forgiveness means that the innocent one accepts the responsibility to release the guilty one. Forgiveness means that the innocent one resolves his or her wrath on the failure of the other by the dynamic of love. To resolve in oneself the pain and burden of another's failure should be done without making the other feel it, for it is not authentic forgiveness if we must first punish the other for their fault! Forgiveness releases the other in spirit, and refuses to hold them captive to the mistake. Forgiveness lays aside any power play.[2]

Forgiveness is especially important in family relations. There is a tendency for spouses to "hold" things in relation to the other as a way of manipulating obligation or competition. Faith-bonding is the key to applying love so totally that it releases the other, actually refuses to put the other in bondage or obligation. It says, "Your problem now becomes my problem."

Only when a person is dodging responsibility to deal with an issue is it proper for us to say, "That's your problem," as an attempt to help them face up to their own responsibility. This is what we call "tough love." But if we say, "That's your problem," to excuse ourselves from the cost of love and caring in working with the person, we violate the nature of unconditional love.

In an article entitled, "How to Experience Forgiveness from the Heart," Gordon MacDonald wrote, "Forgiveness just might be the keystone in the arch of all relationships where loving and being loved is an issue. The failure to give or receive forgiveness probably accounts for the collapse of marriages, families, and friendships."[3]

When your children are small and do wrong, it is easy to forgive them. But what about when they grow to adulthood and make deliberate choices which are contrary to what you believe is right? When, in order to distance themselves from the issue, they say hurtful words to you and do things to further distance themselves from you in defense?

Special friends of ours, former Congressman John and Mary Jane Dellenback, have walked with us in some difficult times. Mary Jane is a professional counselor, and they both have had so much wisdom to offer us. In conversation about family relationships, Mary Jane pointed out that young persons need to take ownership of values as their own. In doing so, those whose family bonding has been the strongest and best may take a large swing away from parental values, but invariably circle back to those with which they grew up. But the choice has become their own. The unfortunate thing is when parents give up on believing in the children and allow anger and disappointments to eat away their spirits. Forgiveness then becomes difficult or even impossible. We have had to discover that it is in our forgiving that an estranged one sees God's forgiveness.

Jesus told Peter that forgiveness is an attitude of heart, the willingness to forgive "seventy times seven" (Matthew 18:22). Contrary to a legalistic limit, forgiveness is to be the openness of love. MacDonald further comments, "To forgive is to withhold judgment, forswear vengeance, renounce bitterness, break the silence of estrangement, to actually wish the best for the person who has hurt us."[4]

To forgive is to express that we are fully aware of how often we need to be forgiven. Paul wrote in Colossians 3:13, "Forgive whatever grievances you may have against one another. Forgive as the Lord forgave you." Faith is modeled by parents as they personally practice forgiveness, and demonstrate positive spiritual disciplines.

Preaching in a meeting of several evangelical church groups, Myron was met by a gentleman after the service who thanked him for the message, but added, "I'm not one of these Christians. I don't believe in this blood religion, in the innocent suffering for the guilty." Myron, still holding his hand, looked him in the eyes and asked if he was married. Upon the man's affirmative answer, Myron responded, "I'm sorry for you, for you can't have a happy marriage, or a peaceful family, or even any close friends."

The man almost bristled, and said, "What are you talking about?"

To this Myron replied, "You just told me that you do not believe in the innocent suffering for the guilty. You are not an angel, you will blow it, and when you do, the innocent will have to suffer for your guilt and keep on accepting you, or you will be a very lonely man. But you just told me that you don't believe in the innocent suffering for the guilty." The man responded, "I'll need to think about that."

At the evening service the man returned, and Myron preached of the cross, God suffering for our guilt—the cost of forgiveness. The man responded to the Gospel that evening with the words, "For the first time in my life I can trust the Christian faith to my lawyer's mind!"

Forgiveness is hard. It is costly, the most costly and most difficult thing in the world. It does mean that the innocent must lovingly resolve their own indignation at the sin of the other and then enable the guilty to be free.

Deed Reaches beyond Word

Faith is not easily explained, but it is evidenced in the way in which we practice our love and obedience to God, the way in which we hold the spiritual and the secular in vital tension, the way in which we live *in* the world but not *of* the world.

In the family, faith is expressed in the freedom and meaningfulness of our communication. Paul Tournier writes of this in a very personal way as he relates the challenge and manner in which he and his wife, Nelly, worked together in a meaningful discipline that included each having time with God. In their shared journaling, in a note that confronted Paul sharply, Nelly wrote of their problem as she saw it, "You see, you are my professor, you are my doctor, my psychologist, even my pastor, but you are not my husband." Paul adds:

> Without equality there is no true communion, and outside of God there is no true equality. I am not thinking of equal ability but of equality as a human being, as a person. That is where equality comes in, different though you may be one from the other. I was an intellectual; Nelly wasn't. I was a debater, an idea person. And suddenly, with one stroke under the inspiration of God, Nelly put her finger on my problem of which I was unaware. It took me months to gain an understanding of it, and years to grasp its full meaning, so sure of themselves are men with their rational ways as compared with the intuitive approach of women. . . .
>
> Ah! How those first years of silent meditation together as a couple transformed our relationship! I also learned how to genuinely listen to my wife. We became one another's confessors and from then on we knew, as nearly as it is possible in this world, each other's most intimate concerns.[5]

In our marriage we have learned much of the same, especially in later years as we have continued to mature together. In the early years of our marriage and family we were too much dominated by trying to do everything right, seeking to shape the lives of our children by being good role models and good disciplinarians. In far too many instances this got in the way of just simply being a loving dad or mom. The pressure to succeed should not be allowed to overshadow the joy of faith, of simply being God's persons together in love.

M. Scott Peck writes, "So it is when we love children, we spend time admiring them and caring for them. We give them our time. . . . The time and the quality of time that their parents devote to them indicates to children the degree to which they are valued by their parents."[6]

Learning Happens in Life's Experiences

Having walked together in love, parenting, work, and various service roles for over forty years, we have learned some things about family that work.

1. We have found it important to discuss our problems candidly with each other. We try to fight fair, dealing with issues rather than putting each other down.

2. We have learned to assess ourselves to see whether the problem is within me rather than first blaming the other.

3. We are confident in our commitment to each other, in our covenant as a foundation for examining our differences, without fear that this will "blow it."

4. We have learned that as we grow and change in life's demands and experiences we need to share our new areas of need with each other.

5. We enjoy friendship with many people, and we assure each other that we do not wonder if we could be happier with some other person.

6. We have learned to pray together over difficulties, and

this is not easy if it is to be authentic and not by rote.

7. We have found the community of believers, our covenant group, and our corporate worship to be essential to our spiritual vitality. They are increasingly a joy and a fulfillment.

We should manifest this joy in *worship* both at home and with others in the gathering of public assembly. We express it in *stewardship* as we evidence our pleasure in partnership with God. We authenticate our faith in *social values* as we select areas of identification and commitment. We articulate this joy in *witness* as we find authentic ways of sharing our walk with Christ. And perhaps above all, there is the virtue of just being there as an *authentic self.* Participating in all of these experiences together strengthens our bond of love.

> To be virtuous is a matter of character,
>   acquired by the disciplines that practice virtue,
>   living in a community that has clear expectations,
>   behaving in a way consistent with who we are
> To be virtuous is to act by a God-enriched character.

A faith in Christ which is a catalyst in family bonding needs to be in constant focus. This is especially true as the children are growing into maturity. We as parents model this faith by living in a way that is consistent with our teaching.

Paul writes to Timothy reminding him that from a child he had learned the God-breathed Scripture so that as a man of God he could be thoroughly equipped for every good work. Paul's words are relevant for us, "But as for you, continue in what you have learned and have become convinced of, because you know those from whom you learned it, and how from infancy you have known the Holy Scriptures, which are able to make you wise for salvation through faith in Christ Jesus" (2 Timothy 3:14-15).

There is a moving and very sad story of Friedrich Nietzsche, the famous nineteenth-century atheistic philosopher whose views in many ways shaped the thought that led to two world wars of this century. As a teenager he is said to have written, "I must know Thee, unknown One, Thou who searchest out my soul and blowest like a storm through my life. I would know Thee and even serve Thee." But apparently he never found the fulfillment of this vision. Later he was asked why he was so negative toward the Christian faith, to which he is said to have responded, "I was never impressed that the members of my father's church enjoyed their religion."

Life Carries with It Accountability

The acceptance of the child, including the infant, in the "covenant family," the church, is very important in the child's faith development. Our expressions of joy in the Lord are caught by the children. At each stage of development a child in the covenant community will be taught about personal commitment to Christ.

In the Anabaptist/Mennonite tradition of faith, our theological interpretation is that the child up to the age of accountability is "safe" in its relation with God. This is to say that there are no "lost" children until they come to the age of accountability, to an understanding of their choice for or against God which they will make for themselves.

This position that in early years the child is "safe," not "saved" as a personal experience of reconciliation to God as a believer, is built both on the simple teachings of Jesus, "of such is the kingdom of heaven," and on Paul's profound theology in Romans 5. Paul implies that a child is "safe" until coming to the age of accountability, for "sin is not taken into account when there is no law." The infant is "safe" until the time when he or she "sins after the similitude of Adam's transgression" (Romans 5:13-14, KJV), that is, by his or her own conscious and responsible decision.

This is not to be construed to say that a child might never

come to a sense of "lostness." Nor is it to say that if a child grows up in a Christian family and always thinks positively about Jesus, this person will never need conversion. The developing person's sinfulness is not primarily in terms of bad things that the person may or may not have done; we should see sinfulness as the deeper level of self-centeredness. It is from this self-orientation that all alike need to be converted to God-orientation.

We parents need to be close enough to our children so they feel free to come to us when they need to talk about personal, spiritual things that may be on their minds. We should not wait for our congregation to hold special meetings as the only opportunity for children to make a faith commitment. Our own faith needs to be consistent and appealing and our relationship with the children open and inviting, so that they will feel free to come to us when the Holy Spirit brings them to this time of God's call.

When Esther was a girl, living in a jungle village in India, most of her Christian teaching and nurture happened the three months she was at home with the family during school break, and the three additional months her mother stayed up in the Himalayas where they went to school. The other six months in boarding offered very little Christian nurture. But she grew up learning what it meant to pray, trust, and serve a real God who loves and Jesus who saves. Her parents modeled the teaching they gave their children. They were persons who prayed much and saw real answers to prayer.

Every evening by lantern light (for they had no electricity within ninety miles), her father would talk about ways in which God had worked in their lives. He would tell stories of our forebearers in the Anabaptist movement of the sixteenth century and how they gave their lives for their faith. He would relate how God answered his and his wife's prayers. He would read from the Bible and they would sing together. But Esther never recalls her parents telling her or her brothers that they needed to confess that they were sinners or make a commitment for baptism. He simply told them that God would call them some day to confess their sins and give their lives to Him.

One day when Esther was nine years old, she made her way from her afternoon nap where she couldn't rest, knowing her daddy was reading in the living room. He saw her coming and reached out as she began to sob. She told him she didn't know what was wrong, but she had been miserable for several days. "I think I know what's happening," he said gently. "I think God might be calling you to give your heart to Jesus." He was close enough in touch with his children and with God so that the Holy Spirit could do His work. They talked about it and he helped her come to Christ. At that point Esther was accountable to God for her life. She was then instructed and in a few weeks was baptized, kneeling in front of the little jungle congregation between two Indians who were also baptized.

Myron came to Christ similarly, by going in from his work at the barn to tell his mother that he wanted to become a Christian. She called the pastor and he came to the house. The three of them sat together in the living room and the pastor explained the way of salvation and then they prayed together. After an instruction class, Myron was one of nine young persons who walked down into a stream and knelt to receive baptism.

Our own children made their commitments to Christ in public church services. Their commitments were genuine and meaningful for them as well. We as parents rejoiced with them, and stood with them in their baptism. It is important that as parents we be close enough to God and to our children to enable them to be free to come to us and let us share with them as they commit their lives to God.

Within the emphasis of our evangelical faith on human depravity or sinfulness, we do not minimize the priority of the imago Dei, of our being created in the image of God. We were created basically good, and sin is a perversion of that good. Our sinfulness is the denial of the primacy of the

imago Dei in our lives, and is an enthronement of self. It is
the ego-centeredness, the center of motivation when life is
self-oriented, which the Scripture speaks of as the heart that
"is deceitful above all things and beyond cure. Who can
understand it?" (Jeremiah 17:9)

Swiss psychiatrist Paul Tournier has described this in a
very helpful way. The unregenerate life is one in which the
ego is at the center and the capital "I," the genuine self, has
been pushed out to the edge. The regenerate life is one in
which Christ is at the center and the ego is pushed out to
the edge. In Christ the genuine self, the capital "I," is
brought back into the center with Christ.

This is a good interpretation of Paul's words, "I have
been crucified with Christ and I no longer live, but Christ
lives in me. The life I live in the body, I live by faith in the
Son of God, who loved me and gave Himself for me" (Galatians 2:20).

Conversion from self-centeredness to Christ-centeredness
comes with the developing child's response to Christ. We
believe infants should be dedicated by Christian parents
with a commitment to bring them up in the nurture of
Christ. This commitment, while usually expressed in the
public worship service in a dedication ceremony, is to a
lifestyle. It means nurturing the child by both private worship and example, and by public attendance with the community at worship.

In the believer's baptism tradition, we hold that children
are *brought* to dedication, but they *come* for baptism. For
us, dedication is not a sacrament securing their salvation,
but the anticipation of their own responsible commitment
when they are of the age to understand and enter a covenant with Christ. As a sign of this voluntary covenant, and of
repentance, the new believer shares in the experience of
baptism.

For believers in other traditions, infant baptism is a sacrament of salvation, but for many others infant baptism is like
dedication. It is a public ceremony of parental commitment

to bring this child up in the fellowship of the church so that at a responsible age the child will make his or her own commitment to Christ. In some churches, confirmation is an occasion of personal commitment.

The implication of a believer's baptism theology is that children are to be taught toward a voluntary commitment to Christ. The child must be given adequate understanding of the Christian faith to support a personal decision. This means that we teach to motivate a decision to become disciples of Christ, and we seek to model this by our own discipleship as parents.

Nurture Unites Home, School, and Church

If we draw an educational philosophy for the home and the school from the preceding approach, we will aim at the children's wills as well as their minds. We will motivate them to see discipleship of Christ as a lifestyle, and to choose this for themselves.

In the guise of being open-minded, some parents say that they will not seek to influence their children in religious decision, but will let them decide when they are mature. This fails to recognize that to avoid giving them adequate religious knowledge is to make it impossible for them to make an intelligent and informed comparison of world and life views. The lack of religious training robs them of the freedom to make an informed decision.

One who decides for or against Christ needs to know the implications of that decision. The choice is made at an in-depth volitional level, not merely at a perceptive level.

Both of our families had a strong faith foundation, a re-source for solving problems as well as giving meaning to life and its relationships. Sometimes the prayers and reading of the Scriptures became somewhat routine; but the experiences were a declaration of commitment. In our families the church was central, providing both spiritual and social resource.

In our own family we have followed the same pattern,

seeking to find freshness in readings with the children and in church involvements. But we were not free of the same tendency for family worship to slip into routine. It is not easy to keep a daily pattern of sharing vital and alive. We look back to some of the difficult times as occasions that bound us together as a growing family.

A family crisis sharpened our awareness of our parental priorities. In December 1957, Myron and his father took our two boys to make a delivery across town. A young woman passing through an intersection did not see the stop sign facing her and drove into the side of our car. The impact threw our car across the street against a pole, giving four-year-old Michael a severe brain concussion. He was unconscious and hospitalized. We were given little assurance from the doctors of how he might come through. But in a deep caring spirit, the late Dr. Powell, our family doctor, spent those nights by Michael's bedside in case he might suddenly need surgery. In response to the prayers of many in our community, on the fourth day Michael slowly regained consciousness. He spoke very slowly and not much above a whisper. "Juice," was his first word.

When the nurse brought him the juice, he looked up at her and slowly asked her a little riddle which he had been asking people before the accident. "Do you know what the doughnut said to the cake?" Excited that he was conscious, she responded, "No, what did the doughnut say to the cake?" He replied, "The doughnut said to the cake, 'If I had all of the dough you've got, I wouldn't be hanging around this hole'!" What a joy! He was all right! His brain was not damaged! He had his memory! We had a time of praise and thanksgiving to God! But during those days of agonizing uncertainty, God brought to our awareness the need to more deliberately bring more vitality and creativity to our family spiritual responsibility.

Recently we ran across the following points that Myron wrote in the back of a book on that occasion. He entitled them, "Lessons from Life":

1. That success in my vocation is not as important as success in raising children for God.

2. That there are areas of life that are entirely beyond human control, and we must rest in God.

3. That rest of soul is not a human achievement, but is brought by the Spirit in answer to prayer.

4. That no price is too great to pay in consecration, that the Lord may be glorified.

5. That things, such as houses, cars, and gain, do not constitute the meaning of life; but rather love in divine fellowship.

6. That the work of God's kingdom and the accomplishing of the divine will and purpose has priority in the Christian life.

7. That faith is victorious when we with small, childlike faith trust our great God.

Faith is learned by example as well as by teaching. As parents model faith it becomes a living expression. Faith is basically response to evidence, for "faith comes from hearing the message, and the message is heard through the Word of Christ" (Romans 10:17). Faith grows or develops in one's life by seeing the evidence as well as by hearing it. Faith arises from mentors as much or more than from lectures! We can say that "faith is caught before it is taught." The eleventh-century theologian Anselm expressed this in his saying, "Faith seeks understanding." But faith would not exist if there was not some evidence of grace, in response to which faith has its birth.

It would be ridiculous to walk through an art museum and stop to look at a particular wood carving—admire its beauty—the lovely form, the warm color, the soft feel of the texture, thoroughly enjoy the marvelous work of art—and then shake your head and say, "What a magnificent sculpture, and to think, there was no artist!" Yes, that would be ridiculous, to say the least. Rather, you take a close look at the sculpture and you see the grain in the wood and you know that the wood came from a tree. You admire the shaping and know that some intelligent person worked at this, and so you look for the artist's name and want to know more about this person. Similarly, faith is a reasoned response to the evidence of God at work, and you want to know more about Him.

One of the more difficult of faith-virtues is trust, with its expression of patience. Benjamin Franklin said, "Nothing is so full of victory as patience. He that can have patience, can have what he will." This statement may be exaggerated, but it emphasizes the need to live with a vision for the future rather than to live with simple wish-thinking. For the Christian, patient trust is grounded in the promises of God, "He who began a good work in you will carry it on to completion until the day of Christ Jesus" (Philippians 1:6).

Faith Is to Be Interpreted

The evangelical community has placed a strong emphasis on integrating Christian faith with education. As Christians we want our children to have an education with the same quality as the best secular program being offered. But we want this education to be more complete, more interpretive and integrative with the whole of truth, than is the case in secular education.

As Christians we cannot be satisfied with an approach which orients life around humanity and its achievements without God. We cannot accept this narrowness of secular thought—"this-is-all-there-is-ism," or "there-ain't-any-more-ism!" We want the child to be open to the mystery and reality of the Creator, Redeemer, and Transformer of life.

Another area of concern is the fragmentation of knowledge that often happens in our educational system as students are asked to achieve in bits and pieces, passing each course for the accumulation of "credits" as though the pieces will eventually constitute a whole. Early in his college administration, Myron stimulated and helped carry through a basic curricular change that had as its special strength the integration of the Christian faith with the whole of the liberal arts curriculum. This led to a more integrative approach to art, history, literature, humanities, and sciences, with theology and a Christian worldview integrated with each.

Partly as an outgrowth of this approach, Myron was involved from the very beginning in the founding of the Christian College Consortium which later led to the Christian College Coalition. Its purpose is to help Christian colleges to offer Christ-centered educational programs. The member colleges teach with a Christian worldview, to integrate the Christian faith in the whole educational curriculum and process, and to develop learning communities in which the mentoring, the lifestyle, and relationships are expressions of the meanings of new life in Christ.

In education, Christian teachers reach for the excellence sought by our academic peers, but we do so because we believe the orders of creation and human fulfillment call us to excellence in an authentic relation to Christ. We also seek to relate scholarly thought to the "sacralizing" of life. Thinking and doing are brought together in "being."

We hold that the truths which we study, when integrated with "the truth that is in Jesus" (Ephesians 4:21), will bring us into a transforming relationship with Truth which is ever confronting us but ever beyond our mastering. We owe it to Christ, to His Church, and to His mission to engage in the most effective way of providing the next generation with evidence that we have carefully thought through an authentic approach to the meanings and values of life.

The wise man said, "Train a child in the way he should go, and when he is old he will not turn from it" (Proverbs 22:6). Our friend Burnett Thompson, a one-on-one evangelist on Capitol Hill, told us of a dialogue with his son during one of those swings away from family values we talked about earlier. His son asked him, "Are you not a man of faith? Can you not believe that your son will sort out the

important things to believe and return to them?" To this
Burnett answered, "Yes, but I'm concerned for you in all of
the things that will happen in your experience between
now and the time that you return to basic beliefs."

Chapter Six
God's Sculpture Means Partnership, Not Control

Husbands, in the same way be considerate as you live with your wives . . . as heirs with you of the gracious gift of life (1 Peter 3:7).

The ego tends to extend itself and, in doing so, seeks to dominate or control others. Ego-centered persons lack the kind of security which allows them to be vulnerable. Secure persons will let others be themselves and relate with them in mutual enrichment. Insecure persons engage in many and various forms of power play. But God sculpts through partnership.

Peter's words are of special note; the *King James Version* says that we are "heirs together." We find this to be the ground for the partnership we enjoy as wife and husband. We are mutual participants in the grace of God. The security of married life is based on the principle of self-sacrifice. It calls for the "lay down your life" demands of love.

In creating an effective sculpture, there is always more than one element involved. The greatest sculptures are the result of the equal working together of spirit, mind, and body, intellect and motor skills, the material form and the aesthetic element. If any one of these components is more dominant, the sculpture will be "stillborn." So it is with the Divine Sculptor's work with us!

There is a quality of art in our culture which is void of meaning. For example, one sculptor who is known worldwide, and who is found on the pages of art history books, went out to a vast desert, drew a long straight line in the sand, then stood at one end of the line and stared at it. Some persons have called this art. But the truth is that it is effective only for the artist himself. This is a one-sided, individualistic, nihilistic experience. Only when the artist brings together himself and the culture in which he lives can art be born.

When God, the Master Artist, works, He brings together the two complementary components, man and woman, and uses them equally in crafting a beautiful sculpture — the family.

God has sculptured the family with man, the muscular protector, intellectual interpreter and family guardian; and woman, the sensitive and intellectual stimulator, child-maker and companion. Both are necessary for the family.

The man is the physical protector and woman is the emotional or "feeling" custodian. The Scripture which speaks of women being keepers at home is the same word as is used for "The Lord keepeth thee." It doesn't necessarily mean, as Esther describes it, "stayers at home," but custodians of the home. Both man and woman are strong, but their strengths lie in different areas of life.

In marriage we are called to be partners in the whole of life. In creation, God made us "in His image, male and female He created them." It is significant that the narrative tells of the creation of man, and then the specific account of God's creation of woman, not from a separate lump of clay but from a rib from Adam's side! This marvelous story shows woman is not merely of "like substance" with man but of the very "same substance!" This could well be a creedal statement, and should be noted by those who want to set up male dominance from the creation account.

Further, this event immediately follows God's directive to Adam to use his creative intellect and to name each of the

animals. It is also then said that there was no animal qualified to be his companion. In response to the fact that there
was no community to be found with the animals, God said
that He would make a helper "meet" or fitting for Adam.
The Creation account presents man and woman in partnership; God created persons appropriate for one another.

The principle of headship is not emphasized in this passage; instead, the emphasis is on partnership. Headship is
later ascribed to the husband as a God-given responsibility
in marriage (Ephesians 5:21-33). This is not a principle of
universal male headship but is a special family principle,
with the meaning of the term being more specifically that of
"guardianship."

Headship as Guardianship

"The husband is the head of the wife as Christ is the head
of the church, His body, of which He is the Savior" (Ephesians 5:23). It does not say, "of which He is Lord," although
He is that, but that "He is the Savior," meaning He gives
Himself for the salvation of the church, for its well-being.
The theological emphasis is not on authority but upon care,
upon guardianship. So the husband is the savior or guardian of the wife and family.

The husband is the head in the responsibility of "caring
guardian" of the wife and family, similarly as Christ is the
head of His church. What a compliment, and what a responsible role! The husband's primary charge is to give himself
for the security, the well-being, and happiness of his wife.
As a precondition for such a relationship, this same passage
calls us to mutual submission in the partnership of marriage, "Submit to one another out of reverence for Christ"
(Ephesians 5:21). This is then repeated in direct address to
the wife in her relation to the husband's role as guardian.

This principle of mutual submission is generalized by
Paul in other writings, especially in the great Christological
passage to the Philippians (2:1-12). We are admonished to

have the same mind that was evidenced in Christ Jesus, for whom equality with God was not something He clutched after; rather, He became human and humbled Himself to serve and to give His life for us. This is to be the spirit in which we serve one another. "Me first" leads to relationships that are superficial.

Some, in simplistic readings of the Scriptures, generalize or isolate one passage from the whole, and thereby universalize the concept of male headship. As a consequence women have been treated with injustice, and have been made to feel that they are second-class persons.

Some schools of thought teach a "chain of command," as the order for family relations—husband, wife, child. This surely is not biblical theology; it comes from a poor hermeneutic that weds a biblical literalism to a social or cultural position. "Chain of command" has been employed to defend male dominance and chauvinism.

The passage in 1 Corinthians 11 which speaks of God—Christ, man, woman—is not to be set in a hierarchical pattern. To do so would imply that Christ is inferior to God, and woman is inferior to man. The theology of the passage is that as God and Christ relate, so husband and wife are to relate (1 Corinthians 11:3).

The Ephesians 5 passage on marriage and family is a marvelous discourse on the mutuality of relationships. Myron emphasizes three aspects of life together:

> We covenant together in our trusting;
> We change together in our sharing;
> We mature together in our loving.

One of Myron's esteemed colleagues, a vice president of the Christian College Coalition responsible for faculty enrichment programs, was elected to be an elder in a Washington church. Upon her election, the pastor, to the consternation of many, changed the earlier position of the congregation which had been to call women as well as men to share as elders. He began teaching against women being commissioned, placing a strong emphasis on universal male headship. He made it very difficult for Karen to be commissioned by the congregation.

One morning she came to work and told Myron of the pastor's lecture to the Session the evening before. He had attempted to find male headship as a universal pattern in his interpretation of the Creation account.

As Myron listened, he began to chuckle. It was Christmas season, and he said to Karen, "On the basis of his interpretation, when I see God I will need to tell Him that He really blew it, for He had no business going to Mary with His plan without first checking with Joseph."

It is of special note that Joseph was apparently still living when Jesus was engaged in His ministry, and yet he kept a low profile in comparison to Mary. That he was still alive is evidenced by the question of the Jews, "Is this not Jesus, the son of Joseph, whose father and mother we know?" (John 6:42)

Women Are Made of the Same Substance

God created humanity in His image, "in the image of God He created him, male and female He created them" (Genesis 2:28).

It is worth repeating that the details in Genesis 2 show God creating woman from the side or rib of Adam, perhaps a symbol of their belonging together. But perhaps more important, God did not select another lump of clay to create Eve of "a similar" substance; He took a rib from Adam and made Eve of "the same substance!" This seems to us to be the theology of our creation. In this "other" each finds the limit and the liberty of life.

In 1 Corinthians we read that man "is the image and glory of God; but the woman is the glory of man" (1 Corinthians 11:7). This says that the creation of humanity in the image of God is God's glory, His full expression of creative goodness. Perhaps from the next phrase, that woman is the glory of man, of humanness, we can say that she is the full expression of human goodness, of that in which man delights.

That husband and wife are partners together is emphasized by Peter in our opening text, in which he refers to them as heirs together "of the gracious gift of life" (1 Peter 3:7). In being partners each one learns to understand and respect the strength of the other. By giving space to the other and encouraging the other, each one is able to function in ways that enrich the relationship.

When two married persons live for the good, the freedom, and the honor of the other, they can truly be heirs together. We talked about the circle, a symbol of love, in an earlier chapter. We see this circle demonstrated in Philippians 2:5-8 where Jesus is described as lifting up God, even though He was "in the form of God Himself." In verses 9-11, God exalts Jesus. In this passage we see a perfect circle of love: God glorifying Jesus, Jesus glorifying God. What a beautiful model for husband and wife.

Peter refers to Sarah "who obeyed Abraham and called him her master" (1 Peter 3:6). A closer translation of the Greek text would simply say that she called him "Sir." We are not that formal in our family. The terms which we use to address each other are much more familiar, but are just as respectful.

The spirit of control will actually kill the sparkle, even the life, of the relationship. Where there is overcontrol, persons will endure rather than enjoy one another. A family should be a place of freedom, of joy, of trust, of enjoyment. This should be true for husband and wife, and also true for the development of children as they grow in freedom to be unique as persons.

Caring and Confronting Enrich Relationships

Partnership in marriage and family indicates that we truly care for each other, that our sharing is that of a mutually enriching relationship. The uniqueness of each is known in honesty and openness, with a caring that is the answer to the prevalent problem of "codependence" in which there is a surrender of uniqueness.

"The feeling of being valuable — I am a valuable person — is essential to mental health and a cornerstone of self-discipline."[1] Being valued and being valuable gives to a child a positive spirit. This sense of worth is something caught early in life, absorbed from wholesome family life, and becomes a part of a person's identity.

A free and cheerful spirit brings a gift of encouragement to another. The story is told of Phillips Brooks, one of the great American preachers, walking along the street on a cold winter day. He stopped to purchase a newspaper from a paper boy. With a smile he said to the lad, "It's a cold day, isn't it?" The boy smiled and responded, "It was, sir, until you came by."

A dysfunctional family exists because of violations of respect for other persons. A healthy family is one in which each and all members are mutually respected. This does not mean there are not differences, or strong personalities confronting each other, but it means that in loving each other there will be a depth of caring that is also confrontive.

John Bradshaw speaks of this confrontation as contact and compromise, and calls us to "fight fair," listing ten rules for doing so:

1. Be assertive (self-valuing) rather than aggressive (get the other person no matter what the cost).

2. Stay in the now. Avoid score-keeping. "You are late for dinner. I feel angry. I wanted everything to be warm and tasty," rather than, "You are late for dinner as usual. I remember two years ago on our vacation you, etc."

3. Avoid lecturing and stay with concrete specific behavioral detail.

4. Avoid judgment. Stay with self-responsible "I" messages.

5. Be rigorously honest. Go for accuracy, rather than agreement or perfection.

6. Don't argue about details, e.g., "You were twenty minutes late." "No, I was only thirteen minutes late."

7. Don't assign blame.

8. Use active listening. Repeat to the other person what you heard them say. Get their agreement about what you heard them say before responding.

9. Fight about one thing at a time.

10. Unless you are being abused, hang in there. This is especially important. Go for a solution, rather than being right.[2]

From our own forty-two years of experience, we would underscore the special importance of the last statement. *We should work for solutions rather than work to prove we are right!* Both of us are strong personalities, and to be in partnership and upholding each other is not always easy. Each of us can be sure we are right! But when we come to terms with the importance of that love circle, we usually find a satisfying solution. We want to reach beyond the issue to renew the love for each other. Love by its nature always reaches beyond oneself to the other. To say no to self enables one to say yes to others.

Former First Lady Barbara Bush said, "It doesn't matter who or where you are, or how successful you become in a worldly way. . . . In a corporate board room, in a hospital operating theater, setting public policy, or managing your private life . . . you must care for other people."

Being positive, taking time to refresh our own spirits, being rested rather than exhausted, giving our best to those close to us—all of this is demanding. It often includes needing a bit of space, at least the practice of "minute vacations" for the health and wholeness of the mind and spirit.

When we are tired we often lash out our frustrations at those we love most. Occasionally, over the years, Esther has reminded Myron that he must have had a difficult day at the office, that his frustration is showing. And there have been many times over the years when Myron recognized this on his way home, and made plans to spend some time back on our little farm, working in the field or trimming our fruit trees. As he cut away with a set jaw and a stroke of the pruning shears, Esther teasingly described him as cutting "this budget item, this project, or that program. It needs to be pruned." He then heads back home released and refreshed.

Another must for parents to avoid, even unthinkingly, is to bring up negative issues with the family at the meal table. Mealtime is not the time to discipline or complain. It can have ill effects on the family. Mealtimes should be some of the happiest times in family life. We are meeting our physical needs and our "togetherness" needs at the same time.

A "Bill of Rights for Parents" Can Build the Family

Two friends of ours, John and Naomi Lederach, Coordinator and Director respectively of Community Education at the Philhaven Hospital, Mount Gretna, Pennsylvania, have written a "Bill of Rights for Parents."

> Ever feel overwhelmed by parenting? The following guidelines may help you put your responsibilities to your family and your responsibilities to yourself in better perspective.
>
> 1. You have the right to make rules. Children must learn that there are boundaries and consequences.
>
> 2. Be different from other parents. Do not let other parents be your standard. You are you and your family is different. Enjoy it.
>
> 3. You can disagree with your children. Don't be afraid of them. Realize that they can also disagree with you. The helpful thing is that you need to know what you stand for and why.

4. Show your feelings, both anger and affection. But you need to realize that you can and should also have self-control.

5. You have a right to make parental mistakes. Remember, all of us as parents do the best we can at any one moment or decision. You can also admit your mistakes to your family. This frees them to admit mistakes to you.

6. You have a right to privacy. There are some things that are yours, and some time that is yours and some places that are yours. Remember, you also need to be alone.

7. You have a right and privilege to have your own friends. Just as your children need friends, so do you. Enjoy this.

8. At times you need other people to help you. You may even want to seek professional help. You do not have all the answers all the time. Realize this and without hesitation ask others for assistance.

9. Lead your family to worship. Do not send your children or family to church, take them. Realize also that you can lead your family to worship in other places, like at home, on vacation, or at a family outing.

10. Keep growing. When any organism stops growing, it begins the process of death. You are never too old to learn about yourself, your family, and most of all about God.

These ten suggestions should help to make your load lighter. Don't use them to be self-condemning, but rather as guidance.³

Mutual Respect Builds Family Harmony

The husband-wife relationship is primarily one of mutual love and respect. It is not one of competitive egos or power plays for dominance. True partnership is mutually enriching and enjoyable. Should one dominate the other and alter the mutuality of the relationship, both suffer loss. Or, should one use the other, serious problems can develop. It is not uncommon to hear a mother scream at her child, "Wait till your dad comes home! He'll beat it out of you," or some such threat. For one spouse to use the other is a sign of personal weakness. It breeds in the child a fear of a domineering, tyrannical father; this then is transposed into other relationships, such as the child's concept of God as Father.

Some spouses intimidate or patronize the other in front of the children. Such behavior robs children of the wholeness the home should provide. This imbalance may create in them patterns that will alter the character of their future relationships.

One problem which readily results from a parental pattern of one-spouse dominance is dependency on the part of the developing child. As a consequence, the young adult may become "so busy seeking to be loved that they have no energy left to love."[4]

In the developing child's adolescent years, it is important that the parents have good communication between themselves, so that they in turn can have good communication with the developing adult. To help adolescents understand and accept responsibility for their potential for creating life is important in these special years.

The more children see Father and Mother respect each other, the more they will respect their friends of the opposite sex. It is this respect that keeps one person from "using" another, and calls them to relate in a manner of courteous regard and of special sanctity. Sacrifice, a central value of Christian living, is essential for a respectful and satisfying relationship. The universal Christian symbol is the cross, and such love includes sacrifice.

There is a story often told by Myron's predecessor in college administration, Dr. John R. Mumaw, a man whom we have highly regarded as a spiritual and professional mentor. It is the story of an occasion when the former King and Queen of England visited the Dominion of Canada and gave marvelous expression of this mutual respect.

They were riding on a flatcar through the streets of Ottawa, the Queen standing on one side waving at the people and the King doing the same on the other side of the car. As they moved along they came to an orphanage on the Queen's side of the car, the bleachers filled with children waving and shouting to get the attention of their King.

The Queen didn't simply wave back, as though "I am the one you wish to see," but she stepped across the flatcar and said something to the King. He turned and walked across with her to greet the children in the bleachers. But instead of just waving to them, he took the Queen by the arm, and with a bow, he presented her!

Chapter Seven
God's Sculpture Includes the Extended Family

A record of the genealogy of Jesus Christ the son of David, the son of Abraham; Abraham was the father of Isaac, Isaac the father of Jacob, Jacob the father of Judah and his brothers, Judah the father of Perez and Zerah, whose mother was Tamar, Perez the father of Hezron, Hezron the father of Ram, Ram the father of Amminadab, Amminadab the father of Nahshon, Nahshon the father of Salmon, Salmon the father of Boaz, whose mother was Rahab, Boaz the father of Obed, whose mother was Ruth, Obed the father of Jesse, and Jesse the father of King David.

David was the father of Solomon, whose mother had been Uriah's wife . . . and Jacob the father of Joseph, the husband of Mary, of whom was born Jesus who is called Christ (Matthew 1:1-6, 16).

The family sculpture includes the extended family, for we are a part of one another in the larger circle of grandparents, cousins, uncles, and aunts. We have photos of four generations on both sides of our family. These photographs are very important to our family.

Five of our children's great-grandparents died before the children were born. Seeing these four-generation pictures of themselves with their living great-grandmothers and great-grandfather gives them a sense of history and of coming from real people who were special.

The Scriptures carefully give us genealogies for good reasons. Myron once met a man in India who told him that he committed his life to Christ upon reading the genealogy of Jesus in Matthew 1, for here he discovered Jesus to be an actual person of history.

God uses the extended family as the larger expression of the multitude of His personality gifts for the enrichment of each family member.

In our travels in Africa we have found some very expressive Makondi sculptures of Tanzania. We purchased several carved in ebony, depicting the extended family, with many bodies and/or faces carved around the block of wood. From the bottom of the sculpture to the top, there is the distinct movement from one generation to another in the extended family. As we stood watching one of the artists, Esther asked him, "All of the Makondi sculptures have a similar and distinctive style. Where do you get your ideas? Do you copy something?" "Oh, no," was his quick reply as he pointed to his head and his heart. "It comes from here and here." The sculptures are visual expressions of one of the most vital aspects of their culture—the extended family.

When Esther begins a sculpture, usually she works from inside out. For most materials the sculpture needs an armature, an inner stabilizing material such as wood, wire, rods, and plaster. Then she applies the clay, wax, or latex to the armature and continues to model it into the final shape. The finished piece follows the shapes of the armature but takes on a quality of its own. The armature gives it stability only while the building process is going on and has some effect on the outer shapes. When the piece is completed, the armature has much less importance, but it is there when wind, rain, and storm threaten the work. God sculptures families that way. The layers of parents, grandparents, uncles, and aunts are the armature, the stabilizing force.

Western modernity has resulted in the nuclear family and

an attitude that freedom comes in not being obligated to any persons beyond our immediate circle. As a consequence many people are social paupers, cut off from their extended family. The American nuclear family must, indeed, find ways to maximize the extended family.

The modern family's problem is not only emotional loneliness, but also a lack of a basic sense of belonging in one's social setting. We all need a group relationship which holds us accountable for the best in our potential and values. True "self-discipline is self-caring," as Peck writes,[1] but this becomes stronger in community and not in individualistic isolation.

The move to the nuclear family has deprived society of the values which are transmitted from generation to generation in wholesome and enriching relationships. We experienced these positive benefits in our family on both sides. This is true in a unique way with Esther's parents who invested nearly eighteen years in mission work in central India. Papa's stories of life and mission in this exotic and romantic setting never ceased to fascinate our children. Much of their early orientation in international awareness came from Grandpa Kniss' interesting and compassionate stories. In this way a people came alive for our family with meanings that were later reinforced by associations with Indian persons and travel to India as a family.

The extended family also provides a deep sense of security. It becomes clear to children that as their parents relate to the grandparents whom they love, so they in turn can relate to their parents with the same understanding. Children participate in the dynamics of extended family relations in ways that often have an unconscious assimilation of values.

Quite recently our daughter, Marcia, who lives in California, was frustrated about how to work with a problem with her seven-year-old daughter, Lara. Lara had been taking violin lessons since she was three years old, and the discipline of daily practice was becoming more of a battle with her mother. She announced one day that she wanted to quit the lessons. She simply didn't have enough time for schoolwork, play, and violin. After a rather stressful conversation or two, in desperation Marcia called to talk to her father and ask what advice he would have for her. Myron reminded her of her own experience at about that age with piano lessons. We gave in too early and allowed her to decide to quit. When she was grown she asked us, "Why did you let me quit? I wish you had made me continue." Of course, Myron wouldn't tell her what to do, but he suggested some ways to make it less demanding and encouraged her to again talk it over with Lara.

Some days later, when we made our weekly call to Marcia, she was nearly bursting to tell us what had happened. She had told Lara about calling Grandpa Augsburger, and the story about her own piano experience. After Lara quietly pondered the story, she said, "Mom, you're a lot older than I am, and you've lived a lot longer than I have, so I'll do whatever you decide!" She is still taking lessons.

The interrelationships of the extended family can be a beautiful networking of support and counsel, for us as well as for our children. It is very important to us. We invite their counsel each time we contemplate major changes in our work, or in little things when we are together, even, "Which scarf looks best with this dress?" or "What did you think of this morning's sermon?" The advice we exchange between ourselves is not merely for help in decision-making, but for the dynamic of reinforcing our need for each other and the caring we know is always there.

Now that we have granddaughters, we are aware of the very special bonding between grandparents and grandchildren. We are finding a new sense of fulfillment in being an extended circle of love for them. Living some distance from each, it becomes a matter of periodic visits rather than the daily or weekly relation that many grandparents enjoy. We have had to find other ways to communicate between visits by telephone and by mail, assuring Caitlin and Lara of the reality of extended love.

Belonging Is Security

Urbanization and professionalism can interrupt family circles, as people live many miles from extended family. In that case they can benefit from a surrogate family in the local church, a fellowship which can provide the dynamics of an extended family for enrichment and accountability. Paul's words to the Romans, "Be devoted to one another" (Romans 12:10), is a key for our relationships in the immediate family and also in congregational family life, a simple but profound statement.

We have observed firsthand the pressures brought to bear on family life from both urbanization and professionalism, patterns which have increased in the last four decades. Coming from a more separatist, rural, and somewhat ethnic church community, we have felt the impact of this change on the church and on our family. In our work interdenominationally, we have found that many groups are just as ethnic as are the Mennonites, and in similar ways have been impacted by these pressures.

Urbanization has introduced many of our people to another lifestyle, and professionalism has enabled them to achieve in this broader world with remarkable efficiency. People move from a close ethnicity to a more open participation. Consequently, each generation examines and evaluates its roots, choosing whether to follow or reject the values it has been taught. For example, we have found that many of our Mennonite youth try other things for a while, but most return to the basic values that they have been taught.

Professionalism has its own unique set of problems. In our family, due to our professions, we often failed to engage our children adequately in extended social resources around us. It is not easy to involve your children in the roles of a college president. As parents we did enjoy the many friendships ourselves, but we needed to find ways to share these with our children. Such relationships should be encouraged for the highest fulfillments in the potential of each child.

Due to roles which caused others in our social circle to

think of us primarily in our administrative position, our children were often robbed of some of the personal benefits of community living. There were times in which teachers and pastors, in seeking to avoid favors for the children of the president of the college, actually backed away from spending equal time with our children. In light of this, encouragement from the extended family has taken on an even more important role.

As we have matured, we have sought to find in our professional roles values which in turn we can share with our family. We also consider it important to increasingly seek ways in which we can enter into their interests, professions, and achievements.

Esther is an accomplished artist, and in addition to her work as a sculptor, she frequently lectures in various parts of the world on the Christian as artist. She has had a special ministry with artists of Asia and Eastern Europe. While organizing an international art exhibition in conjunction with the conference of the International Christian Media Commission in Sheffield, England, it was a special joy for her to invite our son Mike to accompany her to help in framing and exhibiting 140 works of art from some twenty countries. The two weeks of work, fun, and adventure together in England were most memorable.

The two of us are enriched by discussing the theological content and implications of her lectures on a scriptural view of "art, symbol and meaning." This emphasis has helped us to look beyond the particular symbols of our faith to their meanings. It enables us to more freely emphasize the constancy of meanings, even though some of the symbols may change, as we seek to relate the meaning of a Christian lifestyle to a changing culture.

Intergenerational Relationships Build Strength

Grandparents can be the children's best friends. Our children felt that way about theirs. They went to their grandparents often for advice or when they felt discouraged. Grandpa Kniss and Grandpa Augsburger were the kind of good friends our children could count on.

Marcia recently talked about her Grandpa Kniss, who went to be with the Lord when she was in college. She recalled him to be so very caring in a quiet tender way. "He focused on every person who was around him," she said, "and he could tell when I was 'down.' Once when our families were all together—Uncle Mark's family had just come home from India and everyone's attention all day was on them—I was struggling with a difficult problem. Grandpa noticed and took me aside. I could cry on his shoulder and he comforted me."

Their Grandma Kniss is still living. Marcia has always been very close to her. She is almost ninety years old and throughout her life has given herself to hard work in missions. Her love and ministry to others continues, though she is confined to a chair. She has a prayer list which she carefully covers twice each day, rising at 5:30 every morning so that she can pray for each person in the family and others too, by name, before breakfast, and then again in the evening. What a source of strength and encouragement to us all!

This is what being Grandpa or Grandma is about, persons to whom the family can go, knowing they have time and they care.

Our sons went through a time in the '60s, when they didn't adapt well to haircuts! One evening we were at their grandparents for dinner. Mike's hair was especially long and shaggy, as that of so many boys in the '60s. Esther (typical mother!) commented that she wished he would have his hair cut. Grandpa replied, "I didn't notice. I see the boy under the hair!" We were duly reprimanded. The generation gap is often wider between parents and children than between grandparents and grandchildren.

When our sons, John and Mike, were ages four and five, they spent a couple of weeks on Grandpa Augsburger's farm in Ohio while we were in meetings in Oregon. While Grandpa was at work all day, the boys had full rein of jumping in the hay, pretending they were driving on the high seat of the tractor, and gathering the eggs from the chicken house. They loved bringing an egg or two at a time to Grandma at intervals through the day. One day, Grandpa, who was afraid they would break the eggs, wired the gate shut so they couldn't get them. But the boys simply couldn't resist gathering the eggs. They crawled over the gate, filled their little hands with an egg in each and came back to the gate. What could they do with the eggs in their hands? They threw them over the gate first and then climbed over to pick them up—yes, shattered, splattered eggs! What a letdown—and what a lesson!

Grandparents, uncles, aunts, and cousins are each and all a vital part of the extended family. Grandparents especially serve as interpreters of change, and they offer the stability of clarifying and emphasizing meanings from their many years of experience.

Values and traditions, as they are interpreted, are passed on from one generation to another. These values in the lives of grandparents and parents leave to children a life-long treasure. They are a witness to God's presence, that the eternal Sculptor has been at work in His people's lives. In Joshua 22:26 we read concerning the influence each generation has on their children, "Let us . . . build an altar— but not for burnt offerings or sacrifices. On the contrary, it is to be a witness between us and you and the generations that follow, that we will worship the Lord. . . . Then in the future your descendants will not be able to say to ours, 'You have no share in the Lord.' " What a responsibility. When God is the Sculptor of the family, future generations can never say that they had no part in a godly relationship.

The first year of our marriage Myron started a tradition which is still important to us. On Esther's first birthday after we were married, Myron instructed her to sleep in, that he would prepare breakfast. When Esther came to the table, there was a large stack of pancakes, the height of a cake, with a large candle in the middle. Myron proudly explained, "I can't bake a cake, so I made this instead!" Esther says, "It meant more to me than any bought cake."

On Myron's birthday following, Esther fried pancakes. This became a tradition. We had pancakes every time for the children's birthdays, and now they do it for their children!

One time Myron was going to be on a long flight on his birthday. Esther drew a picture of pancakes in her birthday card to him and tucked it into his briefcase. As a coincidence, he was served pancakes on the plane!

Traditions, though they may seem insignificant, can be a sweet spice in the extended family. Due to cultural change, some traditions no longer have the same meaning as they did for great-grandparents. But the extended family offers a context in which the larger group can share in change by the testing or evaluating of lasting values. This is more healthy than to change simply by one generation reacting to the authority of the preceding generation.

As a family we are deeply committed to Jesus' teachings on the way of peace and nonviolence. We seek to take seriously His teaching that we are to love our enemies. In the extended family this has definitely been strengthened by the faith and practice of each of our families of origin, but especially by Esther's father, Lloy Kniss. As Esther grew up, then as our own children came, Grandpa would tell stories by the hour about his experiences of World War I. When he was drafted into the army he was a conscientious objector to military participation. He was very respectful of his country and government, but he refused to wear the uniform or to carry a gun, because they were integral parts of war.

Papa suffered severe persecution, even physical torture in the camp, but he was consistent in his responses to his interrogators and took it with such spirit that he was highly respected. When, after many months, he was given an honorable discharge, he took the train back to his home in western Pennsylvania. The sergeant who had been so cruel to him in the camp had kept informed about Papa's schedule. Learning of his discharge, he made a trip to meet him at the train station in Pittsburgh, where he tearfully apologized to Papa for the violence of his treatment. Papa's story in a little pamphlet, "Why I Couldn't Fight," has made a lasting impression upon us as a family.

As a family we believe that there are two kinds of people in the world: those who will kill other persons and those who will not. With our biblical understandings of the life and teachings of Jesus, and the examples from our extended family and history, we identify ourselves with those who will not take the life of another person. We stand with Dr. Ronald Sider who has said, "I love my country enough that I will die for it, but I will not kill for it." We also interpret our citizenship as Christians that way. Parents rob the next generation if they do not serve as bridges for interpretations which actually engage in thoughtful evaluation.

We need to bridge the generations and enrich one another by common interests. When children grow to be young adults, there is usually some degree of separation or challenge to parents, as the younger persons seek to establish their own identity. This is a necessary experience in personality development. It should be a time when as parents we express our own security and faith that the values taught will bear fruit.

This calls for the strength of patient love, of being there without controlling or determining the other's life. Some changes will be unimportant or inconsequential, while others will wring us out as parents because we know their significance. It is important to know the difference so that we don't create battles where the issue is unimportant.

One view of the generation gap comes from Jerome Goldstein, Boca Raton, Florida, as quoted by Ann Landers in the *Washington Post*, March 2, 1991. It may be overdrawn, since no generation can stand aloof from the way in which we contribute to changes, but here it is:

Don't Blame the Elderly for the Failings of Society.

We are probably the only members of society in the history of mankind for which the younger generation has so little respect and has demonstrated such a shameful lack of regard. Senior citizens are constantly being criticized, belittled, and sniped at for every conceivable deficiency of the modern world, real and imaginary. Upon reflection, I would like to point out that it wasn't the senior citizens who took—

the melody out of music,
the beauty out of art,
the pride out of appearance,
the romance out of love,
the commitment out of marriage,
the responsibility out of parenthood,
togetherness out of family,
learning out of education,
loyalty out of Americanism,
service out of patriotism,
the hearth out of the home,
civility out of behavior,
refinement out of language,
dedication out of employment,
prudence out of spending,
or ambition out of achievement.
And we certainly are not
the ones who eliminated patience
and tolerance from relationships.

Hearing each other, taking time to be together, and finding projects that can be done together can help a family bridge the differences rather than widen the gap. In doing things together, we model the values we hold important and take the time to be mentors. In the extended family we multiply our resources, and we test our values together.

Playing Together Is a Laboratory of Values

As we share in loving relationships, we overcome evil with good. Charity covers a multitude of sins! Our good times together, our play and our work, become a special laboratory for testing our values. In contrast, our lack of time together robs the family of this transmission of values. The Bible suggests the importance of quality time together as mentors for children.

> Hear, O Israel: The Lord our God, the Lord is one. Love the Lord your God with all your heart and with all your soul and with all your strength.
>
> These commandments that I give you today are to be upon your hearts. Impress them on your children. Talk about them when you sit at home and when you walk along the road, when you lie down and when you get up. Tie them as symbols on your hands and bind them on your foreheads. Write them on the doorframes of your houses and on your gates (Deuteronomy 6:4-9).

We enjoyed our growing children, and beyond doing things together we shared the pleasure of just being together as family. True, there were times of stress and of differences between us, but we all knew that we could count on one another's love and support, no matter how we came out. The main problem of spending quality time together was that as the family grew older, we each had a very busy schedule in which we operated. The earlier schedule of running to piano lessons, ball games, and church youth activities with each child was a small problem. As the children grew older and chose other interests, those activities faded and other things moved to the fore.

While spending a one-month sabbatical in Africa and five months in Basel, Switzerland, we took our fourteen-year-old daughter. Each of us became very occupied by the studies we needed to work on. Marcia had taken her high school assignments and books along for the entire term, Esther was doing her master's thesis research, and Myron was engaged in post-doctoral studies at the university. Work became demanding in those months in Switzerland, in spite of our efforts to spend time together.

After a few weeks of this demanding work schedule, Marcia one day handed her daddy a slip of paper (which he still has) with the following excerpt from Peter Marshall:

> God is a God of laughter,
> as well as of prayer . . .
> a God of singing,
> as well as of tears.
> God is at home in the play
> of His children.
> He loves to hear us laugh.
>
> We do not honor God by
> our long faces . . . and austerity.
> God wants us to be good,
> not "goody-goody."
> There is quite a distinction.
> We must try to make the distinction
> between worship and work,
> and play . . .
> less distinct.[2]

We all needed this forthright reminder! To laugh and play together is a therapy of relationship. However, it is not a good idea to laugh *at* one another. Sometimes the distinction between *with* and *at* is not easy to make, as when we found our two young boys up to their knees in a muddy ditch with their neighbor chum, coating each other with mud like live sculptures! Or, in a swimming incident, when mother and children teamed up to give dad a ducking, and in the skirmish mother's and dad's feet collided so hard that it broke her toe. Seeing it bent sideways across the next toe, Myron quickly grabbed it and jerked it straight! We laughed and cried together. We have done so about many things, but we have tried to avoid laughing at one another when there is suffering of deliberate wrongdoing.

As we write these lines we know that we have not laughed nearly enough. Myron especially wishes that he would have learned to laugh more and not carry so much of the weight of caring for others.

To hold worship and work together is one of the more important disciplines of discipleship. This lesson is caught in family life to the degree and in the manner in which parents hold all of life as sacred. Having grown up on the farm, and having been enriched by the many lessons absorbed from his dad while working together, Myron was concerned that he could not share in quite the same way with his children. He could not involve them in his work as college president in the same way as his dad shared with him on the farm. His memories of hours of working together with his dad gave him a longing for similar times with his children.

As the children grew we engaged in hobbies and work projects together, including raising calves to provide funds for the children to go along on a trip to India, returning through Israel and Europe. Later, when the boys were in their mid to latter teens, at their request, Myron bought a building lot, drew house plans, and hired a contractor to provide an additional carpenter to help them learn the carpentry trade. This is a career which John and Mike pursued for some years with remarkable ability and success. They created Augsburger Construction, a building company, and Augsburger Development, as a holding organization for apartment buildings which they built.

However, after a few years John returned to his family counseling role, and Mike developed a flying business, began raising beef cattle, and is presently back in construction. Marcia followed her parents into education as an elementary school teacher, and later became a lawyer. Each of us in our family is uniquely different from the others. We think that is exciting.

For the Christmas week 1992, since our daughter in California could not come to Washington, we arranged for the whole family to spend the days in California. We were invited by Myron's brother David to use his house in Clairmont, and the family was able to be together for nearly a week of sight-seeing, playing tennis, etc. It was a week of fun and laughter, of reminiscing and sharing, a refreshing time in the freedom and love of family.

A good friend, Dr. Robert Lamont, for twenty years the distinguished pastor of the First Presbyterian Church of Pittsburgh, has shared an insight which is very meaningful, as we think of the several generations in our family:

> I am the God
> of Abraham,
> of Isaac, and
> of Jacob. . . .
>
> He is the God
> of differing personalities,
> of varying circumstances,
> of succeeding generations.

The Church as Community Enriches the Family

No one family can experience or express all of the richness of life with Christ. In sharing with others, our faith experiences are tested, enriched, and authenticated. In such a relationship of community, the children have opportunity to see the realities of faith being lived out by persons other than their parents. At the same time, commitment to a congregation of persons walking with Christ holds us accountable as a family in the integrity of our own walk.

As a very young married couple, six months into marriage, we were called to the ministry of the Gospel and to a pastorate in Sarasota, Florida. Myron was twenty-one and Esther twenty. The agents for God's calling were Bishop Truman and Ruth Brunk of New Port News, Virginia, who had responsibility for a newly founded church there. In a special sense of the Lord's leading, Truman drove to Harrisonburg, Virginia one morning, not knowing why, but feeling that God was asking him to make the trip. There he met us at Eastern Mennonite College where we were visiting to arrange for a return to college the next fall. The moment he heard that we were there he knew why he was. He looked us up, presented the urgency of our assuming the pastorate of this new Mennonite church in Sarasota, Florida. After his presentation, and leaving it to our promise of prayerful consideration, he turned around and drove back to his home in Newport News, believing he had heard and obeyed God's voice.

Some six weeks later, after considerable discussion, counsel, and prayer, we felt it God's will to accept the call. This was an enriching experience as we served for a number of years under Truman Brunk's oversight as our bishop. While writing this manuscript, Myron received a phone call from Truman and Ruth, both now ninety years of age, expressing their continuing love and friendship that has been a support and enrichment to us through the years. A few weeks after the call, we drove the four-hour trip to take them out to dinner and to spend some special time together. They have been like parental mentors.

Families are enriched and strengthened when they have a meaningful relationship with fellow Christians in a strong and vital local congregation. Children have traditionally been mere spectators in much of church life "until you get a little older." One example is in the Communion observance. We can remember our children standing there watching curiously (or hungrily) as the emblems were taken. How wonderful it could have been if we had taught them at an early age what the beauty of Communion is and then we together could have partaken in some form of a love feast. Even if they couldn't understand all of the implications, it would have given them a feeling of being a part of the body, the church. This may be in part what Jesus meant when He said, "Let the little children come unto Me . . . for the kingdom of God belongs to such as these" (Mark 10:14).

One of the greater needs in most local congregations is to participate in a God-given community of grace in which each person becomes a participant. Children need the larger circle of faith and fellowship in which they can see, become involved, and test the values being taught by their parents. But the parents need this too, and their sharing helps the children to develop with them. The Strommens, in *Five Cries of Parents,* designate four areas where the larger group strengthens the parents:

> Helpful support groups
> Esteem-building activities
> Positive belief system
> Insight into self.[3]

As a small boy, Myron was strongly influenced by his great-grandfather, Bishop John M. Shenk, who often spent time with the Augsburger family and who "at a ripe old age" died in their home. Being six at the time of his great-grandfather's death, Myron's memories are quite clear. On the last weekend of June 1992, a Shenk reunion was held at Harrisonburg, Virginia, with nearly 500 descendants present from across the nation.

This wing of Myron's family could trace ancestors back to a castle prison in Thun, Switzerland, where nine generations ago a great-great-grandparent, Melchoir Brenneman, was imprisoned for his Anabaptist faith. To follow this line down through the history of families in America was enriching. The gathering proved to be especially significant for the middle-aged and young adults who found fresh meaning in reviewing their roots, and recognizing a family line of faithful Christians of the same denomination down through many generations.

During one session together, Myron's brother David, a professional counselor, arranged a group of family members in a living sculpture to show how people or clusters of people make up various types of family formations. The demonstration helped the larger circle present to identify and understand relational values and/or problems that affect us all. It is in the extended family where values are most fully tested and where loving acceptance and encouragement is shared.

When Myron was researching for a presentation in memory of Bishop Shenk, a significant statement from his diary impressed us. It was written on his sixty-second birthday, January 19, 1910:

> It is with a feeling of deep gratitude that I take my pen to jot down a few thoughts on this birthday. It is surely a blessed thing to just unreservedly give ourselves to God and ask Him to take full control and full possession of us and direct all of our affairs, looking to Him constantly for His directions and for His transforming power to make us more and more like Him.
>
> I have been given a positive promise this day that the Lord shall be my God and I will walk in His ways and keep His statutes and His commandments and His judgments and hearken to His voice (Deuteronomy 26:17-19), and the Lord has given me a positive promise this day that I shall be one of His peculiar people and to make us high above all nations which He hath made; in praise and in name and in honor; and that we should be an holy people unto the Lord our God as He hath spoken, and my prayer is that I might walk worthy of the Lord unto all pleasing being fruitful in every good work and increasing in

the knowledge of God; strengthened with all might according to His glorious power unto all patience and long-suffering with joyfulness.

And I do this day make a new consecration to God by placing myself, my family, my friends, my church, my possessions, my all upon His altar to be used according to the good pleasure of His Will. "Thou wilt keep him in perfect peace whose mind is stayed on Thee."

This heritage of faith has obviously influenced his many descendants. Among this group, made up of persons in a variety of churches and denominations, an amazing number have followed in ministry in the church, and the others work and professional roles of others reflect the same spirit. The transmission of godliness from generation to generation is a primary role of the family.

Each family needs to share with a congregation of believers the higher calling to be members of Christ's body. In this relationship with the larger family of faith, children experience the meaning of covenant in its greater socio-spiritual dimensions. From the very early dedication of a child, the larger circle of the congregation pledges to support the parents in bringing the child up in the nurture of the faith and in the benefits of public worship.

Being disciples is not only a matter of things that we do, it is a spirit of devotion to Christ. To share enriching worship is just as vital in our calling as Christians as to share in evangelism or social ministries. We not only call one another to Christ, but we live together in the fellowship of Christ. It is in worshiping together, praying together, singing together that the family is motivated to walk faithfully with Christ.

During a recent visit of our daughter and granddaughter from California, we drove from Washington, D.C. to Harrisonburg, Virginia, where we had lived for twenty-two years, and where our daughter had grown up and been involved in the church and community. She wanted to visit friends, but especially to attend the church where she had been baptized. Commenting later on the worship experience of hymns, solos from the *Messiah,* and the sermon, she said that she had the distinct impression that the people there enjoyed a more quiet piety, expressive but not excessively so, a piety with which she was comfortable. Our conditioning does affect the manner in which worship symbols and styles involve us.

Forms of worship vary, and may actually need to be changed at different times in order to meet needs and circumstances in our lives. But in whatever form, the reality of meeting God must be authentic for the worshiping person. The following lines, adapted from St. Anselm, have been a meaningful expression of the personal nature of worship:

Lord, help us —
    to seek Thee in longing,
        and long for Thee in seeking;
    to find Thee in loving,
        and to love Thee in finding;
    to worship Thee in joy,
        and enjoy Thee in worship.

Chapter Eight
God's Sculpture Matures Us in Sharing

Each one should use whatever gift he has received to serve others, faithfully administering God's grace in its various forms. If anyone speaks, he should do it as one speaking the very words of God. If anyone serves, he should do it with the strength God provides, so that in all things God may be praised through Jesus Christ. To Him be the glory and the power for ever and ever. Amen (1 Peter 4:10-11).

A number of years ago, Esther had several pieces of sculpture in a group art exhibition in Virginia. At the opening of the exhibit, the artists were invited to be present so that viewers might meet them. During this time, Esther noticed a blind man enter, led by a friend who stopped and described as best he could each painting and sculpture, helping the blind one to "see" things through his eyes. When they got to Esther's abstract wood sculpture, the friend picked it up and handed it to the blind gentleman. He stood there for a long time in silence rubbing, feeling, and turning the piece over and over. With reluctance, his friend urged him to move on in order to "see" the rest of the exhibit.

Before they headed for the door to leave, Esther overheard the blind man say, "Please take me back once more to that wood sculpture." Esther was rewarded for the many, many hours of carving and sanding that went into the piece by this man's pleasure.

This is how God, the Master Sculptor, feels when He sees His family sculpture bring joy to others. In the movie *Chariots of Fire*, Eric Liddell said, "When I am running, I feel God's pleasure." So Esther says, "When I am sculpting, I feel God's pleasure." And when the family brings pleasure to others, we too can feel God's pleasure.

When God sculpts the family, He calls us not only to enjoy togetherness, but also to reach outside the family and bring joy and comfort to others. This brings God pleasure. The spirit of caring is vital to our life together.

We do not grow in the social graces by being hermits or by living selfishly. Growth comes by interaction with, and looking out for the needs of, others. We also grow as we participate with others in testing the values of life and in choosing to assimilate into our lives the values we have seen lived out by others.

Sharing Means Selectivity and Prioritization

What we call *values* are learned primarily by sharing in the selectivity of life. The choices parents make, the things for which we are willing to sacrifice, the decisions about social engagements, and the priorities in our stewardship all work together to express our values.

Values are seen in—
    the high regard in which we hold persons,
    the refusal to misuse people,
    the style in which we relate to others,
    the rejection of all racism,
    the absence of class distinctions,
    the refusal to gossip or degrade another,
    the freedom and spirit in which we share love.
These express our values of personhood.

Selectivity is not only a matter of choosing between the good and the bad, but also choosing different levels of the good. It has been said that most of our choices are between the good, the better, and the best! That means that we can avoid mediocrity and engage in a more magnanimous style of life. However, it is important that these choices be seen as finding the best for us, as we pursue our own personal development. This is not a matter for competition, seeking the better over other persons.

Changes that compromise values are usually brought into a person's life in association with people who reject godly values. Peer pressure among people who are involved in compromising values is an intense influence today. Individuals in compromise are in need of support from others, and consequently they place a lot of pressure on their associates. Teenagers find peer pressure one of the most difficult "authorities" to resist. Even when reacting against authority from their homes, they fall prey to this new authority. For a family to have lines of authority and respect, rather than a dogmatic authoritarianism, it is essential to spend quality time together.

In many ways children reflect parents and extended family members who have been their mentors. While there are similarities in looks, in speech, in expressions, in posture, in gait of walking, etc., which are basically hereditary, there are also overlapping characteristics which are learned or developed in family environment. These two interact with each other. The two are not exclusive, as in the old story of a lad who came home from school with a very bad report card. He was very fearful of showing it to his parents. Suddenly he got an idea, and running up to his dad, he gave him the report card, and said, "Isn't it just terrible? How in the world do you explain it? Is it heredity or is it environment?"

When our granddaughter Caitlin was about four years old, Myron broke his arm when the ladder on which he was standing broke, while he was painting a gable on our house. His arm needed surgery to put a plate on the bone. As Caitlin's mother, Jan, was taking her for a visit to the hospital, Caitlin insisted on stopping at a supermarket to buy him a present. When they arrived at the hospital, she handed Myron three gifts—a roll of LifeSavers, a box of Band-Aids for his arm, and a picture she had drawn of him lying in bed with arm outstretched. In his arm was a plate, with knife and fork! In her limited understanding of what had happened, her gifts were well planned. And, best of all, they were full of love and caring. They are now tucked away with other gems of family love.

Family sharing makes a home into a "seminary of life," a school of values and spiritual realities. In the family we bring the sacred and the secular together. We need to balance the sacred and the secular, to interface the two without losing either. The best preventive for problems in children is to provide them a home in which they know that they are loved and trusted. The home offers the child a sense of security, social values, an understanding of the importance of generosity, and especially a knowledge of God. At home we establish the core of life from which the perimeters will then be set.

Family Sharing Should Reach out in Service

Our calling as Christians is first in *being* before it is in *doing*. Our mission is above all to be a people of God together. We are to be a family in love, in faith, in trust. Too often, as we have found with our calling to the ministry of the Word, there is a tendency to put church work ahead of everything else and to equate this with putting Christ first! But knowing Christ is to walk with Him, to serve Him in serving others.

Dr. Anthony Campolo tells of three things that were prominent in his mother's nurturing. "First, she was always there. Second, she believed in me and helped me to believe in myself. Third, she modeled for me what missionaries are supposed to be." Later, as a sociologist, he learned that what we think of ourselves is to a large degree determined by what the most important person in our life thinks of us. For Tony, this was his mother, who often said to him, "Remember! You can go over the top for Jesus!"[1]

God's calling for each of us is to put Christ first in our lives. But this is not synonymous with full-time work in the church. Church work is at a different level than our commitment to Christ. To put Christ first means personal holiness, family wholeness, relational integrity with all peoples, excellence in occupational roles including one's profession in church work, community and national citizenship, etc. But many church workers have been put in bondage on this matter, by the impression that putting Christ first in life is synonymous with putting church work first! Not so.

Friends of ours, the Peter Wiebe family, lived in a small town in Kansas where Peter was pastor of a church. He tells the story about an evening when he was out on the lawn tossing the football with his sons. A neighbor walked over and said, "Peter, since you aren't busy, I'd like to talk to you a bit." Peter stopped playing and the two began to talk, while he watched his sons look at each other in dismay, take the ball and walk away. Peter said, "I should have told him, 'Not busy? I'm busier now than at any other time.' " The Wiebes moved out into the country to have more freedom and privacy for family time!

A story from our family is similar. One Sunday at lunch Myron promised to read stories to our children in the afternoon. While they were sitting in the family room together, the children snuggled against him eagerly listening, the doorbell rang. Esther opened the door to a gentleman who asked to talk with Myron. She told him that he was not available just then. After considerable insistence he left. Meeting Esther again years later, he expressed his deep resentment that she had not called Myron to the door.

He said, "I knew that Myron was there, for I saw him sitting on the couch reading to his children, and he was not busy!"

Esther didn't give in, but said simply, "Oh, but he was very busy. He had made a promise to the children that he would read to them. This commitment was as important to them as his commitment to anyone else. I'm sorry you couldn't speak to him." Now we wish that there had been many more times when we put family life ahead of pressures from our work in the church.

Family and community need to share in a partnership of mutuality. The pressures of society cause many children to be "jigsawed" into puzzle parts. But healthy families can be the effective blocks in building a new community. As Christians, we are especially qualified to make a positive contribution through the family to the social order in which we live. But whatever our privileges, they should be accepted in humility and never in haughtiness.

Setting priorities of importance in life is a very important aspect of decision-making. Families can help one another to more careful selectivity. Not only does this help to save time, and to use our energies wisely; it also helps us discern what projects or activities are a liability rather than an asset in the long-range view of life.

We Are to Share the Values of Social Justice

In the July 23, 1991 issue of *USA Today,* the "Quotelines" included the statement of Lafayette Williams, a ten-year-old child from a Chicago housing project: "If I grow up, I'd like to be a bus driver." These words, "If I grow up," are expressive of the insecurity of many children in our modern world. This is especially true in the violence of an inner city culture.

It is too easy to take social ills lightly, until they touch our own lives or families. The call of Christ is for us to carry an evangelical or "good news" sense of social responsibility for the family's mission in society. From our own twelve years of living in Washington, D.C., we have learned the difference between inner city life and suburban life. How easy it is for persons to live in the suburbs and never really feel the plight of their city neighbors.

One illustration of how readily we create distance from problems is shown, in that when marijuana was a problem of the "under class" the street name for it was "weed." But when the "upper class" began to use it, the name changed to "grass." Interestingly, society even seeks to reflect "class" in our addictions! We are called by Christ's own example to a compassionate caring for persons, all persons alike, within and beyond the family.

> Values are person-centered;
>   not simply a framing of laws,
>   nor an articulation of codes,
>   nor the exertion of social pressure.

> Values are the enrichment of life;
>   unqualified respect for persons,
>   uncompromised refusal to manipulate,
>   commitment to influence rather than to control.

Life is not measured by the accumulation of things but by the enrichment of mind and spirit. One significant aid in overcoming the gap between the "haves" and the "have nots" is to recognize the full value of each person. There is often more sin in plenty than in poverty. Parents do their children a disservice when they instill a feeling of superiority over others on the basis of plenty.

Maturing is a process, and it cannot be programmed. There is a cumulative aspect to life's experiences which enhances the maturing process. But there are also stages or levels of experience. Reading Bishop Fulton Sheen, we found something that has been helpful. He said that in the very early years, the important thing for a child is personality development. Later, in the secondary level, the significant thing for the child is delineating moral values. These two areas of development are basic if the young adult is to be free and secure and selective in social relationships. And they are foundational for the young adult at the collegiate level who is interpreting and integrating life values. Convictions for truth become evident in this integration of faith and learning.

Charles Finney, the evangelist who was active in the abolitionist movement, gave invitations in his meetings for persons to commit themselves to stand against slavery, and spoke pointedly to the issues of social justice. He affirmed that "social renewal is hindered by persons who fail to take a stand on any issue of human rights." We need to hear this word again today, when many conservative minds are closed to engaging matters of social justice and human rights.

Children are not born with prejudice against persons of other races or economic levels. They are taught prejudice by adults who are significant to them.

When Myron challenged a friend who worked in the White House to help the conservative politicians with whom he worked to promote justice, peace, and human rights he was told, "Just as soon as you use those words you are no longer a conservative!" But these are biblical concerns, and this illustrates the relevance of what we have come to call "A Third Way," being neither rightist nor leftist, but advocating the way of the kingdom of Christ. This way gives us the freedom and responsibility to select from either and to confront each position with the way of Christ. This calls for an informed mind and an authentic commitment to Christ.

Maturity Means Intensity without Stress

We have been enriched by reading the devotional books of E. Stanley Jones through the years. He gives us an interesting outline which he gained from his own extensive reading.

Pavlov, the great scientist, at eighty-seven giving advice to youth, said there were three necessary things:

1. Gradualness. Don't be in a hurry. Take each day as it comes, step by step.
2. Modesty. Do not be proud; be humble in the presence of fact.
3. Passion. Remember that science demands of a man all his life. Be passionate in your work and in your searchings.[2]

For too many of us, life lacks zest, lacks a great passion. It is plagued by the ubiquitous problem of the laziness and intellectual apathy of "couch potatoes." We need to believe so sincerely that this believing will give to life a passionate focus. A focus, or sense of purpose, will keep life from being too diverse. But such a passion should be a motivation, not an obsession, for the latter will only induce stress, deplete energy, and spoil relationships.

One of our friends, Jim Fairfield, is a free-lance writer from Harrisonburg, Virginia. He has said, "Stress can make life miserable. When one person in the family suffers from stress, everybody suffers in one way or another." In his discussion of stress he shares a simple yes or no test in a "Stress Questionnaire" designed to be helpful in self-analysis:

1. My job is killing me.
2. I can't pay my debts.
3. I'm being sexually harassed.
4. I can't find work where I live.
5. I'm drinking to get over my bad days.
6. I don't feel like doing anything.
7. I'm in a bad relationship.
8. I feel driven all the time.
9. I can't get to sleep.

After you give your yes or no answer to each of these questions, you will have some sense of the degree of stress in your personal life. As a proposal for dealing with stress,

Fairfield gives us three steps: Learn to relax, Get in touch with your body-self, and Work to change the problem. If you pursue these thoughtfully, prayerfully, and openly with persons close to you, you will initiate healing changes.[3]

We need to be careful lest the very normal practice of transference in childhood be carried into adult life to support avoidance. Too often in adult years, persons still use transference to avoid dealing with a problem. In marriage there are many forms of avoidance to escape solving a problem together. With significant insight, M. Scott Peck says, "Problems do not go away. They must be worked through or else they remain forever a barrier to the development and growth of the spirit."[4]

It is important in character development that we focus more on *being* than on *doing*. As we think of values, we should above all emphasize the value of the person. We are so performance-motivated that we often fail to be character-oriented. By our example more than our words, we as parents should express the high value we place on the person and on character.

It is said that the measure of one's life is not its duration but its donation. This was expressed by the preacher-poet, Edwin Markham, as he wrote of Abraham Lincoln, "There was a man to hold against the world, a man to match the mountains and the seas."

Families need to take it as a primary mission to develop persons who are inner-directed, who are at peace with God and themselves, and who know the secret of trust in their covenant relation with Christ. To be in the world but not of the world, as the Scriptures teach, can cause tension unless one is at rest in relationship with God and committed above all to His will.

Character Is Formed Early in Life

One of the more unique and dynamic aspects of character formation is what we might call "imprinting." This is an impact of primary and creative structuring in a person's psyche. We use the word "mentoring" to describe the ongoing process, as we recognize that parents, siblings, relatives and friends are all mentors. A very high percentage of what children learn in the earlier years is caught from examples around them. They are great imitators, of style, of expression, of language, of habits, of accent in speech.

Imprinting has been illustrated in very remarkable ways in animal and bird life. Our family inherited from Myron's dad the hobby of raising swans and Canadian geese. It has been learned that if a Canadian goose nest is elevated by placing a ply-board under it and raising it off the ground so that the little goslings must jump down when they hatch, it imprints them for their future nesting habits. When they mature several years later and build their own nests, they will place the nest off the ground so that their goslings will jump down. They have even been known to build nests in old tires that were placed on the roofs of houses to test this imprinting.

Social workers tell us that nearly all cases of spouse abuse and child abuse occur in families in which one or both of the parents grew up in homes with patterns of abuse. A friend who has been a professor for years at a local university told Myron of growing up in Appalachia. He observed his dad, who was on welfare, walk downtown each day and sit on a bench to swap stories with his cronies. As a lad he concluded that his own adult life would follow the same pattern of welfare and loafing with friends.

In contrast, many workaholics have been mentored by parents who seem driven to produce. This latter may have been of necessity to support a family, especially if they were shaped by the Depression or their lot in life was meager and demanding. It is a mark of maturity to move from drivenness to disciplines of selectivity and the resultant freedom of responsible scheduling.

Imprinting is a dynamic challenge in parenting. Dorothy Law Nolte, a family life educator, has shared the following lines entitled "Children Learn What They Live."

If a child lives with criticism,
    He learns to condemn.
If a child lives with hostility,
    He learns to fight.
If a child lives with ridicule,
    He learns to be shy.
If a child lives with shame,
    He learns to feel guilty.
If a child lives with tolerance,
    He learns to be patient.
If a child lives with encouragement,
    He learns confidence.
If a child lives with praise,
    He learns to appreciate.
If a child lives with fairness,
    He learns justice.
If a child lives with security,
    He learns to have faith.
If a child lives with approval,
    He learns to like himself.
If a child lives with acceptance and friendship,
    He learns to find love in the world.[5]

A family is not an island in the sea of life; it is more like a city of refuge in society. There we find the deep satisfaction in a relationship of acceptance even when we have blown it. It is a place of love when we feel the weight of failure. It is a place of hope when we are tempted to despair.

The Christian home is a special unit of love and integrity in a world of sin. It is a place of security as well as of faith and purpose. While not making the "News," our many families who share love, trust, encouragement, worship, and mission together are the strength of our society. They stand in sharp contrast to the absence of love and faith as expressed in the account reported in *Time*, April 8, 1991, of the twelve-year-old girl in New York City who abandoned her baby boy in a trash compactor!

She had lost her parents at four, lived with her aunt in Brooklyn, grew up amidst gangs who settled their drug disputes with automatic weapons. Her cousin had sex with her on several occasions, and she became pregnant. After giving birth to the baby in the early hours of the morning, she stuffed him inside a plastic bag and threw him down a garbage chute, and did the only dignified thing she knew — she went off to school.

But she was sick. . . . At the same time a porter at the housing project turned on the motor of the trash compactor, and hearing a baby cry, turned it off, crawled into the machine, and found the baby in the mound of garbage, and took it to the hospital. A miracle for the little life, but what a comment on our society!

Marriage is a setting in which not only children are brought to maturity. It is a relationship in which the couple who share their love and family responsibilities grow together, to mature in the social, material, and spiritual aspects of life. We have found in walking together for forty-two years that we are better persons through relating to each other! Even difficulties which we have faced together have enhanced our mutual understanding, our prayers together, our sense of what is important, and our support of one another. Family is a covenant of love in which we mature together.

Family Should Provide Hope as a Special Strength

One of the greater ministries to our society is the building of stable and enjoyable family-life situations. The answer to abuse, incest, overcontrol, and manipulation is found in the principles of love and integrity to which God calls us. Home is where one can turn for understanding and for support in the crisis experiences of life. In the Christian home, love, trust, faith, and discipline all merge to create a wholesome relationship.

But home is also where each person should find a friendship that allows total honesty and assurance of acceptance.

The Christian home is where one can come with an anticipation of inclusion in love and faith, a place that extends forgiveness for one's failures.

Home is where we build a passion for hope, where we enable one another to always try again. This is hope for moral engagement, hope for actual possibilities of success, hope to implement the meanings of God's kingdom, and hope to live as disciples of Christ in a world with problems. This hope is not blind, not an escape, for we are realists. We recognize problems and face them:

-spiraling inflation,
  -deterioration of family life,
    -eroding moral and spiritual values,
      -declining support for the poor,
        -disillusionment with politics,
          -resurfacing of racism,
            -resistance to feminine equality,
              -consumption and pollution of natural resources,
                -religious revival without social critique,
                  -technical temperament without spiritual sensitivity.
                    -selective pluralism, limiting reference to Christ.

But we are saved in hope (Romans 8:24), and transformed by the realities of God's purpose; and it is in a broken world that we are called to be "salt and light." We are to be a community of the redeemed amidst the world's fallenness. The Christian family is a seminary of nurture in life experience. And this doesn't end when the children marry and leave home.

After a number of years of difficulty in his life, one of our sons experienced a remarkable change in coming back to the values of his earlier faith. During this time, Myron sent him the words of a Bob Dylan song, which our son knew well. He found these very personal words in the song especially true to his own experience.

"EVERY GRAIN OF SAND"

In the time of my confession, in the hour of my
deepest need
When the pool of tears beneath my feet flood every
newborn seed
There's a dyin' voice within me reaching out some-
where,
Toiling in the danger and in the morals of despair.

Don't have the inclination to look back on any mis-
take,
Like Cain, I now behold this chain of events that I
must break.
In the fury of the moment I can see the Master's hand
In every leaf that trembles, in every grain of sand.

Oh, the flowers of indulgence and the weeds of
yesteryear,
Like criminals, they have choked the breath of con-
science and good cheer.
The sun beat down upon the steps of time to light
the way
To ease the pain of idleness and the memory of decay.

I gaze into the doorway of temptation's angry flame
And every time I pass that way I always hear my
name.
Then onward in my journey I come to understand
That every hair is numbered like every grain of sand.

I have gone from rags to riches in the sorrow of the
night
In the violence of a summer's dream, in the chill of
wintry night,
In the bitter dance of loneliness fading into space,
In the broken mirror of innocence on each forgotten
face.

I hear the ancient footsteps like the motion of the sea
Sometimes I turn, there's someone there, other times
   it's only me.
I am hanging in the balance of the reality of man
Like every sparrow falling, like every grain of sand.[6]

As Earl Burnies, a professor of literature, has said, "A poem is an invitation to explore, not a duty to explain." So we explore in word pictures the scenes in which we see ourselves reflected. As we explore, the important thing is, as Dylan says, that we "see the Master's hand."

In our own family experiences it has been painful but very rewarding to work through times in which family members going their own way, have violated their faith, and then to see them turn again to God and find in Him the forgiveness and joy of openness and fellowship. For us as parents, it is a wonderful thing to realize that God works in ways that will help each child have a very personal faith, not one borrowed or second-hand. And this reminds us that the last chapter of our lives—and theirs—is not yet written!

Chapter Nine
God's Sculpture Incorporates Equity and Mutuality

Make my joy complete by being like-minded, having the same love, being one in spirit and purpose. Do nothing out of selfish ambition or vain conceit, but in humility consider others better than yourselves. Each of you should look not only on your own interests, but also to the interests of others. Your attitude should be the same as that of Christ Jesus (Philippians 2:2-5).

Esther's sculptures have most frequently been cast in molten bronze. But we have also referred to a process in which a bonded casting is made, with bronze powder mixed with two bonded acrylic substances which provide the body and strength for the bronze powder. In this bonding, with the mutual contribution of each part, the sculpture has its strength. More recently a new material of acrylic and marble powder has been developed in which the bonding is so total that the product appears as marble. It is so durable that it is projected to last 2,000 years! It is the mutual interplay that results in the sculpted strength.

God sculptures the family with the ingredients of mutuality. We are built together in His love, and we are strengthened by the mutual interaction of each person in the family. In this union, this interdependence of covenant is our lasting strength.

The last thirty-five years have ushered in a new awareness about the impact of families on personality formation. While it's always been known that our families of origin deeply influence us, we're now discovering that the influence is beyond what we had imagined. We now understand that families are dynamic social systems, having structural laws, components and rules.[1]

Seeing the family as a social system means for us that we show respect for each other and support one another with genuine mutuality. With love there is a reciprocity, a giving and a receiving in return, a spirit of humble interdependence which finds joy in mutual enabling. Love delights in the other. Love, Paul writes, looks beyond oneself to the well-being of others (Romans 13:9-12).

Merton and Irene Strommen emphasize four essential elements for a close family life:

Parental harmony
Parent-youth communication
Parental discipline or control
Parental nurturing[2]

These essentials are first the responsibility of the couple called together to begin the family. God's original plan for family was not a man controlling a woman nor a woman controlling a man. God's plan is for a partnership in which wholeness makes the couple invincible in their love and integrity. This equity in respect and relationship is passed on to the children as security.

Parents are to be models of mutuality. It is in sharing that each person is made the better, for in giving we receive, and in loving we are made the more complete. In this awareness we find a new level of selfhood. Mutuality rather than control makes one the stronger, for in mutuality we receive as we give.

Mutuality Means Serving Each Other

As Christians, our delight is in what we bring to each other in encouragement and enrichment of life together. We must take seriously Jesus' teaching on serving one another. This is His answer for the power struggle between the sexes that too often becomes so detrimental to marriages. We are partners, serving together. The principle of service is expressed in His words, "Whoever wants to become great among you must be your servant" (Mark 10:43). This serving role begins in family. Malcolm Muggeridge wrote of this in his unique style.

> Jesus proclaims His kingdom as the antithesis of power; as a kingdom of love. Pilate and Herod and the Sanhedrin all operated in terms of power; so, on an enormously greater scale, did Caesar; but Jesus Himself disdained power, scorned it, found wisdom in babes and sucklings, and picked His disciples among fishermen. Nonetheless, it is He, not the others, who is remembered, whose birth, ministry, death, and resurrection have provided the greatest artists, writers, composers, architects, with their themes and their inspiration. Without power, He was almighty; with power, the others, like fireflies, shone a while and then disappeared.[3]

A power play intimidates, seeks to dominate, and tends to produce a sense of inadequacy in others. Rather than helping persons develop, we too often engage in power games to control or we use others for our purposes. But not everyone can be the dominant person in a relationship. Consequently some must find their satisfaction in other than a dominant role, lest they feel defeated. Some must find other ways of satisfying their ambitions or inner drives, lest they feel shamed as underachievers. There must be a better way—the way of mutuality!

The strong, aggressive, dominant personality needs to be especially modest, for such patterns are difficult to live with. Marriages are destroyed not only by infidelity; they are also destroyed at the heart by violating the equity of love. True partnership happens where there is a spirit of mutuality, a genuine delight in each other and in one another's achievements. Partnership is the better way!

Myron tells the story of two men in a flea market, one of whom spotted an old lamp on a table. Picking it up, he rubbed it and a genie appeared, "One wish, Sir." The man said, "I would like to be the smartest man in the world." The genie said, "Granted," and disappeared. The other man looked at his companion in amazement, grabbed the lamp and rubbed it. The genie appeared again and said to him, "One wish, Sir." The man looked at his companion and said, "I want to be smarter than the smartest man in the world." The genie said, "Granted," and turned him into a woman! There are, of course, better ways to achieve equity.

Mutuality Develops through Stages in Marriage

There are stages or passages in life and in marriage. There are also levels of fulfillment in a marriage relationship that fall into basic categories.

1. There is the early level of complementary relationships in which we begin our marriage. The focus is primarily on what each finds in the other, which is often centered on the sexual and emotional aspects of marriage.

2. Next, we move to the more full-orbed meaning of companionship where we become authentic partners, best friends. Communication has reached a level of mutual understanding, often beyond words.

3. The third level is that in which we walk together in a more parallel fashion, in which each spouse has a fulfilling role, but ideally not in tension or competition with the other.

4. And fourth, there is the level in which both have the freedom to pursue their respective roles with healthy self-fulfillment, respecting each other's professional roles without trying to control the other. Myron's brother, Dr. David Augsburger, has written effectively on this subject, especially in his book *Sustaining Love.*

Families may suffer from the professionalism of our day which tends to place spouses in very different roles and circles of relationships for eight or nine of the best hours of each day. Unless a couple understands the dynamics of these relationships, and deliberately works on supporting one another with understanding and the security of love, the result can be the breakdown of the family fidelity and joy. When spouses are in professional relationships which relate them closely to other persons, the married couple actually needs each other the more. Family members need to seek intimacy, security, and maturity at each level of their relationship.

Family Is a Support Structure

Bradshaw sees the crisis of the American family related in a large way to compulsion:

> we have a hundred million people who look like adults, talk and dress like adults, but who are actually adult children, driven by shame which fuels compulsivity, and compulsivity is the black plague of our time. We are driven. We want more money, more sex, more food, more booze, more drugs, more adrenalin rush, more entertainment, more possessions, more ecstasy. Like an unending pregnancy, we never reach fruition.[4]

But in the Christian family, where the disciplines of faith and the harmony of God's grace give joy in life and in each other, we experience the freedom "to be." In the healing of grace is a wholeness, love, and openness that is satisfied with life itself. This sense of worth arises from qualities of life rather than exercises of acquisition. When children witness mutual support between their parents, they, in turn, will be enabled to bring to their own relationships a vital complementarity. They will recognize Dad's logic and practicality, if those are his gifts, but they will also respect Mom's insightful readings of motivation and relational dynamics. In mutual respect there will be mutual love, security, and encouragement.

> Family is life together,
>   enjoying one another,
>   belonging,
>   a social center,
>   the orientation of each to life,
>   meeting the demands of sharing,
>   supporting without supplanting.
> Family is life in mutuality.

The greatest support is not in material things, but in the spirit and encouragement needed to face life and to make right decisions. This includes helping young adults to cope in a self-disciplined way with peer invitations to drugs, drink, and sex. The family can provide a basic personal security, an expectation of value-guided decisions, and a sense of worth that will sustain the young adult in times of adverse peer pressure. Loving understanding is the great strength that parents bring to young adults in times of temptation.

Adolescence is a special time to help a teenager to become mature emotionally. It is crucial to avoid shaming and to provide security. It is a time in which the question, "Who am I?" needs to be answered by a sense of personal worth. The Strommen team lists "seven goals an adolescent intuitively seeks to achieve during the teen years."

1. Achievement. The satisfaction of arriving at excellence in some area of endeavor.

2. Friends. The broadening of one's social base by having learned to make friends and maintain them.

3. Feelings. The self-understanding gained through having learned to share one's feelings with another person.

4. Identity. The sense of knowing "who I am," of being recognized as a significant person.

5. Responsibility. The confidence of knowing "I can stand alone and make responsible decisions."

6. Maturity. Transformation from a child into an adult.

7. Sexuality. Acceptance of responsibility for one's new role as a sexual being.[5]

Mutual support provides not only incentive but sustaining encouragement to excel nobly. It is important that the motivation be for the development of the person's whole life, rather than to win over others. Yet, we are engaged in winning, and there should be a motivation to strive to win honorably. The greater reward is in the knowledge of having performed by the highest values and with the noblest spirit. Family is the setting for nobility, a quality of being that permeates each person with honor and worth.

> Our families are the places where we have our source relationships. Families are where we first learn about ourselves in the mirroring eyes of our parents, where we see ourselves for the first time. In families we learn about emotional intimacy. We learn what feelings are and how to express them. Our parents model what feelings are acceptable and family authorized and what feelings are prohibited.[6]

As parents we model what it means to live in supportive roles, to enjoy a relationship of respect and encouragement. This calls for "wise reticence" to treat one's wife or husband with courtesy. It is not easy to be supportive as one spouse to the other, when one always claims to know better! Or think they know better.

Dr. Cecil Osborne, founder of the Burlington Counseling Center, discoverer and developer of Primal Integration Therapy, says, "Every marriage experiences tensions. It is impossible to live in the same house with another person in such a close relationship without problems arising." Osborne relates what he calls the most important decision that he and his wife made, the clarification of agreements for their marriage relationship.

> 1. We agreed that we would never try to change each other.
> 2. We agreed that we would not try to control each other.
> 3. We decided that we would never criticize each other, no matter what the provocation. It seemed at first as though this had cut off a great deal of our communication, so we added a fourth factor.
> 4. We agreed that whenever either one of us was displeased, we had the right and even the obligation to say, "I am displeased or unhappy whenever you do a certain thing." That comment simply sends a message, but does not demand that the other make a change.[7]

Mutuality Resolves Tensions

In the family, children should be able to observe respect shown between their parents, including the way in they handle tensions. They learn not only from the words but from the tones, gentle and patient or cutting and sharp. From this example, they learn how they are also to respect others. In the tensions of family, it is important that children discover "how to fight fair." They will also learn the meaning of compromising in a proper way, compromise that demonstrates that the other person is more important than the issue.

But as children mature, so the relationship between parents and children must change to meet different needs. The development from childhood to young adulthood calls for adjustment on the part of parents to communicate with them as responsible, thinking adults. Maturing children should begin to find in the parents their very best friends. Consequently, when they are asked, parents can be respected counselors in relation to work and relationships. The Strommens comment, "We can help our adolescents find a sense of significance, but not by controlling them."[8]

There is wisdom in the statement of the Jewish father at his son's bar mitzvah, "Up until now I have talked to you about God. From now on I will talk to God about you."

The play, *Fiddler on the Roof*, gives us insight into what it means to be willing to let our children make their own choices. This letting go is much more difficult when we have grown up in a strict setting. Those of us who come from a long historical tradition can relate well to Tevye. He sees that the fiddler on a slanted rooftop is unstable and insecure, and he thinks about how we all need stability and balance.

Tevye sings out his answer to this need, "Tradition!" We are all fiddlers on the roof! Because of our traditions, we can understand who we are and to whom we belong— which is good. But, when faced with his daughters wanting to break tradition in the choice for marriage, Tevye says in resignation, "On the other hand. . . . " We all need to be flexible enough with our children to sometimes be able to say, "On the other hand. . . . "

Maturing children cause change, but the relationship does not end when the children marry. While no longer a parent-to-child pattern of responsibility, the adult relationship calls for ongoing parental support. Parents should fully include the spouse of their married child, and relate in loving support of the new union. At times this may well include the encouragement that comes from very tangible assistance in meeting financial needs. Too many parents hold back this financial assistance until the reading of their will upon death. By then the children may have had an overload of stress affecting their marriage or their confidence. To wait until death may be too late, or the children may no longer need help.

Material and/or occupational achievement by a young couple is not always possible without some parental assistance. It is important for children to learn early to manage material things, to experience the demands of work and saving, the disciplines of forgoing some desires in the present for greater benefits in their future. But in today's economy it is important that parents consider helping their children wisely, lest an undue financial burden limits them in a life vocation.

As parents, we have shared with the family in material things. We have agreed together that it is better to help our children when they are young adults, rather than to make them wait. Handled carefully and responsibly, this may be more advantageous than leaving benefits to them only in our will. And when we did revise our will, we sat down with our children and discussed with them our current plan. We found agreement on our plan to draw up our will with five equal divisions, one share each for our three children, one share for Christian missions, and one for Christian higher education.

We Need to Avoid Perfectionism

Another subtle problem parents often foster in children is to give the impression that they are demanding perfection. Too many men and women struggle with the feeling that they could never please their dad or mother. The problem may be the unfulfilled life of one or both parents who want a child to excel at something they did not achieve.

Bradshaw speaks of the tyranny of needing to always be right. The serious problem of the perfectionist role is enslavement by something imposed on one. As Christians, we must recognize that our identification with Christ is not an imposed perfectionism, but is rather an inward, fully owned relationship which we must work out in expressions that are our own.

One of the greater dangers of life, as E. Stanley Jones writes, is "to set up goals that are unattainable and then go into a tailspin of depression and self-condemnation if these goals are not reached—and reached to perfection."[9]

True, Christ sets high goals for us but, as the Scriptures tell us, He will not give us goals which we are not able to reach. We should have high goals for ourselves, even for one another, but the goal should stress faithfulness ahead of perfection, or we will suffer the paralysis and frustration of perfectionism. Myron's friend Bruce Larson has said, "Perfectionism will drive you up the wall!" And again, "You can't be all right and be well."

Leo Buscaglia provides us with words from an eighty-five-year-old man who just learned that he was going to die.

If I had to live my life over again, I'd try to make more mistakes next time. I'd try not to be so . . . perfect. I'd relax more, I'd limber up, I'd be sillier than I've been on this trip. In fact, I know few things that I would take quite so seriously. I'd be crazier, and I'd certainly be less hygienic. I'd take more chances. I'd take more trips. I'd climb more mountains. I'd swim more rivers, and I'd watch more sunsets. I'd burn more gasoline. I'd eat more ice cream and fewer beans. I'd have more actual troubles and fewer imaginary ones.

You see, I was one of those people who lived prophylactically and sanely and sensibly, hour after hour and day after day. Oh that doesn't mean I didn't have my moments. In fact I'd try to have nothing but wonderful moments side by side. I've been one of those people who never went anywhere without a thermometer, a hot water bottle, a gargle, a raincoat and a parachute. If I had it to do all over again I'd travel lighter next time.

If I had my life to live over again I'd start barefoot earlier in the spring and I'd stay that way later in the fall. I'd play hooky a lot more. I'd ride more merry-go-rounds. I'd smell more flowers. I'd hug more children. I'd tell more people that I love them. If I had my life to live over again. But, you see, I don't.

Many Christians are driven by subconscious perfectionism that results in their failing to enjoy life or one another. In too many cases we hold expectations over one another in the family and fail to accept and love one another just for being there! Unfortunately, most of us learn this too late.

Another aspect of this problem of perfectionism is the stifling problem of parental overcontrol. This was mentioned earlier as an attitude that may arise between spouses. In relation to children, it usually arises out of the insecurity or fear or the pride of the parents. Overcontrol is hard to live with. It robs the developing child of the freedom to be his or her own self, to make mistakes, to learn from those mistakes, and to take ownership of one's own decisions.

Our family has always enjoyed swimming. It was a necessary part of every trip — stop for the night where there was a pool.

Marcia was extremely fearful of the water in swimming pools up until age four. One winter afternoon, I was sitting in the family room while four-year-old Marcia played on the floor. After a while she came to me and said, "Mommy, when summer comes, I'll be able to swim. I have it all figured out in my mind." I replied, "Oh, that will be wonderful. How do you think you will swim?" "Look," she replied as she pulled the footstool to the middle of the room, "this is the way I will swim." And she dived off the stool onto the carpet with motions of swimming. The next time we went swimming I was prepared to play along the edge with her as before, but Marcia jumped into the pool and took off like a fish! The test for me came a few days later at a pool. There was a high diving board that even I wouldn't venture on, and the first thing I knew, Marcia was out on the end of the board shouting, "Watch, Mommy!" I thought I would have a heart attack. I screamed, "Come down, right now!" only to be reminded by Myron to let her jump! I couldn't bring myself to watch, but she successfully jumped in, then and many times following. Protective Mother could have built fear and uncertainty into Marcia, had it not been for Myron's wisdom.

Parental controls may keep a child in good order while the relation and pattern of control is experienced, but once the child has moved out and the control is not present, the inability to make responsible decisions and to follow through can be a major problem. We should remember that as parents we are to work ourselves out of a job! We are to enable our children to make wise decisions on their own.

Responsibility Enables Happiness

Maslow's hierarchy of needs points us to achievement in all the levels of fulfillment. Beginning with physiological needs, he moves to needs of safety and security, then to love and affection, next to the level of self-esteem, and finally to the level of self-actualization.

Many persons spend most of their lives at the first two levels, with the third to some degree perverted by the tendency to self-interest. A more limited number reach the level of wholesome self-esteem. Far too few actually engage the level of self-actualization.

Self-actualization means that we accept responsibility for being what we are and for what we express in our endeavors and relationships. We refuse to blame others or circumstances for where we are. As Christians, we can take the initiative and move ahead, expecting in faith that God will be there walking with us.

Happiness doesn't simply come to us; it is the result of

our maximizing the meaning of life and finding happiness to be a reward. In a real sense, happiness is serendipitous. It is a benefit granted to those who find the full meanings of life.

In the March/April 1991 issue of *The Marketplace,* a unique publication by a Mennonite Christian business and professional organization, there is a list of twelve tips for happiness taken from *Working Smart.*

1. Live a simple life. Simple is better. Don't clutter up your life with too many things.

2. Spend less than you earn. Stay out of debt. Save money. Practice self-denial and patience.

3. Think positively. Fill your mind with useful, uplifting thoughts and images. Read, listen, and watch very selectively.

4. Be cooperative. Resist the common tendency to want things your own way. Yield to the other person more often. Try to see another point of view.

5. Be thankful. Form the attitude of gratitude. List your blessings. Be glad for your opportunities.

6. Make your moods. Cultivate peaceful attitudes. Rise above your feelings. Talk cheerfully.

7. Be generous. Help others whenever you can. Give your time and money to worthwhile causes.

8. Maintain good motives. Work for the good of others, not just yourself. Avoid selfishness.

9. Practice the Golden Rule. Always try to treat others as you would like to be treated.

10. Live one day at a time. Make the most of today. Take time to enjoy life.

11. Learn to relax. Take time to restore yourself. Exercise. Get a hobby.

12. Maintain balance in your life. Devote the proper amount of time to all aspects of your life: spiritual, family, community, career, physical, mental, material.[10]

It is important that we each have patterns of disciplines in our personal lives, for these will enable us to live happily together as families. In this happiness there will be openness, respect for the other, and the encouragement to be one's best in mind and deed, to think carefully and choose wisely. We should seek to be supportive of each other. Rather than emphasizing our differences, we should recognize that we are more alike than different.

We Need Courage to Be Authentic

Our own children remind us that we taught them from childhood to think for themselves. They ask us to understand their mistakes by being aware that they have been *their* mistakes, made by thinking their way through life! It takes courage to risk, especially when children feel that they need to break out of some of the more ethnic characteristics of their cultural heritage.

Yet, by training children to think for themselves in a Christian context, we as parents can have confidence that the values of the Christian life are so meaningful that the children will ultimately choose them. Often this means returning to them even after having tried other lifestyles. This is our faith as Christian parents, that the children will come to see the value of the Christian faith for themselves. This is not just wishful thinking, for it is grounded in the conviction that "He who began a good work in you will carry it on to completion until the day of Christ Jesus" (Philippians 1:6).

Believing in the supreme value of life in Christ and the continuing work and presence of the Spirit, we can trust God to lead our children to the meanings of life in His grace, not because they are our children, but because of divine grace, because of God's call, and because of the superior quality of His love and holiness.

What Paul wrote in his letter to the Ephesians is especially relevant for the family, that we are to "prepare God's people for works of service, so that the body of Christ may be built up until we all reach unity in the faith and in the knowledge of the Son of God and become mature, attaining to the whole measure of the fullness of Christ" (Ephesians 4:12-13).

Responsible living is something in which we share as a family, all at different stages, but each alike in relation to Christ. The remarkable passage that emphasizes this is Jesus' teaching on the relation of the Vine and the branches. "I am the Vine; you are the branches. If a man [or woman] remains in Me and I in him, he will bear much fruit; apart from Me you can do nothing" (John 15:5).

This word picture reveals that true life and nurture all comes from the Vine. Translated into our idiom, this mutual sharing with Christ becomes an encouragement of commonality. Further, we recognize that in parental relations with children, responsible living is not optional, but is a necessity of personal faith, evidencing the relationship the parents have with Christ.

There is a rather personal poem by Edgar Guest that expresses this truth in a singular way.

> I'd rather see a sermon than hear one any day,
> I'd rather one should walk with me than merely show the way.
> The eye's a better pupil and more willing than the ear;
> Fine counsel is confusing, but example always clear;
> And the best of all the preachers are the men who live their creeds,
> For to see the good in action is what everybody needs.
>
> I can soon learn how to do it if you'll let me see it done,
> I can watch your hands in action, but your tongue too fast may run.

And the lectures you deliver may be wise and true;
But I'd rather get my lesson by observing what you
do.
For I may misunderstand you and the high advice
you give;
But there's no misunderstanding how you act and
how you live.

When I see a deed of kindness, I am eager to be
kind.
When a weaker brother stumbles and a strong man
stays behind
Just to see if he can help him, then the wish grows
strong in me,
To become as big and thoughtful as I know that
friend to be.
And all travelers can witness that the best of guides
today
Is not the one who tells them, but the one who
shows the way.

One good man teaches many, men believe what they
behold;
One deed of kindness noticed is worth forty that are
told.
Who stands with men of honor learns to hold his
honor dear,
For right living speaks a language which to every
one is clear.
Though an able speaker charms me with his elo-
quence, I say,
I'd rather see a sermon than to hear one, any day."

Chapter Ten
God's Sculpture Provides Unique Freedom

There are different kinds of gifts, but the same Spirit. There are different kinds of service, but the same Lord. There are different kinds of working, but the same God works all of them in all men. Now to each one the manifestation of the Spirit is given for the common good.... All these are the work of one and the same Spirit, and He gives them to each one, just as He determines. The body is a unit, though it is made up of many parts; and though all its parts are many, they form one body (1 Corinthians 12:4-7, 11-12).

A piece of sculpture which copies another is almost worthless. One of the important qualities of art is that it is uniquely original and one of a kind. Esther, like many sculptors through the ages, casts limited editions of many of her sculptures. However, she works on every piece of a given edition at the wax stage before casting and again at the final finishing stage. Though each piece may appear to be the same as the others, every sculpture is original and different. They are all a part of the same family—the same edition—but all unique.

Each person is an original! We know that when we look at our two granddaughters. While we see some similarities, each has her own wonderful personality and unique gifts and abilities. We are all created in the image of God, but we are not alike. In family we recognize and respect that uniqueness, just as we also recognize similarities of the biological and environmental conditioning that have shaped us.

Each of our three children is uniquely different. If we would use word pictures to describe their personalities, we could say that John is like a steady, deep, quiet river flowing calmly and beautifully along, and that's good. Michael is more like a meandering stream. He sees so many different possibilities in life that he enjoys trying them all and does them quite well, and that is good. Marcia is like the swift, gushing river that we saw in Kulu Valley, India—white with foam from the speed, and heading unstopping toward where it is going. She is much like her father—you can't stop their energy for life. They are both high achievers, but get there in their own unique ways, and that's good. Are we proud parents, or what? Really we are trying to illustrate their uniqueness, but parents' pride in their children is good and wholesome.

As God sculpts, His sculpture changes with the different periods in a family's life. The circle becomes larger. With the second and third generations, the family becomes more expressive of the different roles and patterns within the family structure. There develops an interlacing of circles as the extended family grows.

It is in family that we are to grant each one the freedom of being his or her own unique self. Uniqueness should develop without fear that there will be a lack of acceptance. Family is where each one knows, "This is where I belong, where I am accepted, and where I am encouraged to maximize my particular personal potential." The relationship is one that "leads to peace and to mutual edification," as Paul wrote (Romans 14:19).

In the early years of our pastoral ministry in Florida, a friend who worked with Myron shared his concern about his family. He came from a large family of twelve children, and half of them were actively participating in the church and the other half were not. His father had said to him one day, "I don't understand this. I handled you all alike." Our friend's comment to Myron was simply, "That is the trouble. We were not alike, and he should have met each individual with understanding on his and her own ground."

Each individual is his or her own person, created in the image of God, with the uniqueness that God gives in a rich variety of personalities. This uniqueness is very important in one's self-identity, and should be fully respected and developed by parents and teachers.

For example, too frequently a second or third child has a problem going to the same school where an older sibling has attended, especially if the older one has been a high achiever or strong personality. Or too often, because of the parents' identity and image, children are stereotyped and not given the freedom to achieve of and for themselves.

Uniqueness Makes Room for Selfhood

A family sculpture expressing the family structure will in some way reflect the different placement of children in the family, showing the sequence and relationships that affect their development. But the sculpture should also show the unity that can be known in the diversity of personalities.

We have said that love is not divided when one child enters the family, then a second and a third. There is enough to love each one fully. Just so, respect for the uniqueness of each and their particular gifts is enhanced by seeking to influence each one, in fairness to them, as unique persons.

Further, as each person's uniqueness is respected, a family avoids unwholesome competition. There is no room for a competition which calls each to achieve in life by comparison with the other siblings. Recognizing the unique characteristics of every child will avoid the unfair and crippling competition.

We delight as family when each one excels in the role and gifts which God has given them. We have sought to model this in our marriage. Myron excels in preaching, theological reflection, and practical management. Esther excels in social grace, care and nurture of others, and in creativity through her work in art. Each one enjoys personal gifts but also enjoys and encourages and finds fulfillment in the special gifts of the other.

As the years have passed, we as parents delight in the gifts and achievements of our children, and now, for the past seven years, of our granddaughters, Caitlin and Lara. This is especially rewarding, as we share the excitement of the unique development of each one's gifts.

Marriage Is Complementarity

Married couples often have complementary personalities, and may appear to be at odds with each other. We should not see our differences as problems but as challenges to grow together. When the differences become difficulties, we should not think that we married the wrong partner, but that we have not let the complementation process grow after marriage. A couple is bonded in covenant by God, but each person needs the partner for the maturing process, as they move toward wholeness of relationship.

It is said the highest divorce rate in America is in the third year of marriage. This may be in large part because of the illusion of "undying happiness." Each couple needs to discover the rewards of cultivating happiness in a maturing marriage. But in our Western society, it is said that in nearly half of the married couples, one spouse is in his or her third marriage!

Every couple needs a correct understanding that marriage is a process. This process includes the cultivation of love, expressions of kindness and good feelings, and affirmation of one another as valued and unique human beings.

As we have seen earlier, the price of genuine intimacy is costly. We need to recognize that in the most intense relationships, two people do not give up their own uniqueness, but rather must affirm their distinctiveness. The process of marriage is the continuing affirmation of each other's uniqueness in the relationship. Novelist George Eliot's question is relevant, "What do we live for, if it is not to make life less difficult for each other?"

Marriage is not blending two persons into a common unit; we do not remake one another into our own image. Rather, we provide space and respect for each one to express the uniqueness that God granted to his or her particular personality.

Love gives acceptance, not judgment. Love doesn't live by struggling for dominance. Abigail Van Buren comments, "People who fight fire with fire usually end up with ashes!" When love is altered by the dominance of one smothering the other, the fire of love dies.

As discussed earlier, the most significant aspect of our uniqueness is our maleness and our femaleness. The understanding of one another in this regard, and the respect for the particular qualities each brings to a family is vital to its fulfillment. While we are bonded in Christ with the reality of equality, we are still individual and unique persons.

Personhood Is Freedom to "Be"

As Christians we have a deep sense of the "oughtness" that accompanies our sense of values in life. However, these values need to be understood and assimilated into our lives by authentic choices. We must recognize our freedom, even with its risks, if we are to maintain a healthy mind-set. Family therapist Virginia Satir speaks of the natural endowment of five freedoms:

1. The freedom to see and hear (perceive) what is here and now, rather than what was, will be, or should be.
2. The freedom to think what one thinks, rather than what one should think.

3. The freedom to feel what one feels, rather than what one should feel.

4. The freedom to want (desire) and to choose what one wants, rather than what one should want.

5. The freedom to imagine one's own self-actualization, rather than playing a rigid role or always playing it safe.[1]

Bradshaw comments in this context, "Functional parents will also model maturity and autonomy for their children. . . . The children are then free to grow, using their powers of knowing, loving, feeling, deciding, and imaging to get their own individual self-actualization accomplished."[2]

Each person is in process of differentiation. For this process of individuation and differentiation to proceed, a family needs to offer security and stability. We must recognize that every person needs self-worth, self-acceptance, and self-love. The developing person needs a structure that is clear enough to risk individual growth. A very basic element of this individuation is the spiritual awareness and calling that leads the person to God.

Family is the school of people-making, and this includes each member. Paul wrote, "There is neither Jew nor Greek, slave nor free, male nor female, for you are all one in Christ Jesus" (Galatians 3:28). While maleness and femaleness are realities, Paul says the Gospel of Christ removes the barriers and places women with men in the church as equals, with respective rights as children of God (Galatians 3:26).

In this expression Paul affirms each of our places in terms of roles shaped by our sexuality. He does not place women in a passive role, for he says they are to "learn" with modesty and not seek dominance. In a culture where only men were worthy of literacy, he said women are to learn (1 Timothy 2:11-12). Women are considered co-laborers in the Gospel (Philippians 4:3), and women serve in various roles in the work of the church including leadership roles, as shown clearly in his recognitions of such in the conclusion of his Epistle to the Romans (16:1-16).

Further, the roles of maleness and femaleness do not in themselves determine the gifts of the Spirit given graciously to each (1 Corinthians 12 and 14). Nor is the exercise of those gifts sexually determined, even though their function may be culturally conditioned as we view the kingdom work across the world.

There is a remarkable book, *Call Me Blessed*, by Faith Martin (Eerdmans, 1988), which interprets the Bible as seeking to release us from the determinations that arise from a masculine viewpoint. The book is extremely helpful because it enhances the position of the Christian woman without the negativism of the secular and militant liberation movement.

In Martin's book we are helped to read the Scriptures with realism and honesty, with the respect for God's sovereign acts in creation and sovereign purpose in the community of faith. This "quality community" is created as He pours out His Spirit upon all flesh, including our sons and daughters (Acts 2:17-18).

Family is the setting in which uniqueness and equality can and should be demonstrated. When parents seek fulfillment for each other with their respective potential, and together seek the fulfillment of life for their sons and daughters, there will be a holy joy in one another.

Discipline and Respect Can Be Joyful

Someone has said, "Joy is the chuckle of the soul!" It brings a positive spirit into the most demanding experiences of family life. Discipline itself, if it is to avoid crushing this joy in the family, should be primarily positive. It begins with the discipline of our own lives as parents, and is to be modeled by parents as well as exercised in parent-child relations.

In his book *Dare to Discipline*, Dr. James Dobson calls on parents to reinforce the values of our Judeo-Christian heritage by the careful disciplines that will incorporate these values into the child's life. This is very important, and is to be done with love and respect for the person and worth of the child.

As young parents we needed to learn to discipline ourselves not to exercise discipline on one of the children when we ourselves were angry. Living in the inner city we saw firsthand a lot of painful happenings to children, particularly in the supermarket. We could shed tears with children whose mother or father scream at them with a hard swat across the face, sending them sprawling onto the floor. Is there any wonder that when those children grow to their teens they do the same to others, but with guns? To be effective the discipline needs to be a clear, positive directive for the child's life. When it is necessary to exercise discipline as a form of punishment for some wrong, it should be done with fairness and limited severity, so that the child's spirit is protected from humiliation. Discipline must respect the person.

There is an old story of a man doing the grocery shopping for his wife. He had their little son in the basket of the cart, and the little fellow was crying forcefully. A lady heard the man saying, "Keep calm, Albert; don't raise your voice, Albert; don't make a scene, Albert." Later she was at the checkout counter when the man came, cart piled high with groceries and the little fellow bawling loudly. The man was saying quite emphatically now, "Keep calm, Albert; don't make a scene, Albert; don't raise your voice, Albert." She said to him, "Sir, I'm amazed at how you keep talking to your child like that when he doesn't pay any attention to you." He replied, "Lady, you don't understand. I'm Albert."

Some people speak of breaking a child's will. We regard this as a very dangerous concept. Each one needs to have his or her will surrendered to God's will, that is true, but not broken in the sense of being destroyed. A child needs to use the gift of volition, or will, in right decisions. It is the rebellion and stubbornness of spirit in one's will that needs to be conquered. This is not always easy to discern. As parents, it is not a matter of our conquering the child's will in relation to our own. Rather, we should help the child to master his or her own will by a surrender to the gentle Holy Spirit. As children grow in understanding, we pray that they will surrender to the greater will of God! Discipline should shape but not destroy uniqueness.

Paul writes to fathers, "Do not exasperate your children; instead, bring them up in the training and instruction of the Lord" (Ephesians 6:4). When discipline is administered in love, it will never abuse or humiliate the child. Such discipline will encourage the child to do the right, to become more responsible, positive, and trustworthy. As we share the disciplines of courtesy, of work, of worship, of prayer, of thankful deeds, of respect for others, we will grow together in the will of God.

In the Christian family we respect one another, parents and children, male and female. In doing so, we hear the promise of God in mutuality, "I will be a Father to you, and you will be My sons and daughters, says the Lord Almighty" (2 Corinthians 6:18). This calls for mutual respect, forgiving grace, and encouragement for the next steps in our maturing and in our life together.

Myron's great-grandfather, Bishop John M. Shenk, often quoted a poem which expresses this need for grace.

> He came to my desk with quivering lip—
>   The lesson was done.
> "Dear Teacher, I want a new leaf," he said,
>   "I have spoiled this one."
>   I took the old leaf, stained and blotted,
>   And gave him a new one, all unspotted,
>   And into his sad eyes smiled:
> "Do better now, My child!"
>
> I went to the Throne with a quivering soul—
>   The old year was done.
> "Dear Father, has Thou a new leaf for me?

I have spoiled this one."
He took the old leaf, stained and blotted,
And gave me a new one, all unspotted,
And into my sad heart smiled:
"Do better now, My child!"[3]

Life is more than systems of thought, more than ideas we are committed to live by in some deliberate fashion. We are called to be God's children; we are owned by God. Life has heart and soul. There must be passion to life, zest, something worth living for and something to be excited about.

This becomes very personal, for we are not copies, not clones of one another. As we have seen, each person is an original. But this zest for life is not just to celebrate being unique; rather it is to express one's self in freedom and joy.

Each Person Has a Unique Role

When Paul was converted, he became a unique addition to the Church of Jesus Christ. His training at the feet of Gamaliel with the equivalent of a doctorate in historical theology was quite different than Peter's academic level of a bachelor of arts along with John and their colleagues, earned by their discipleship of Jesus of Nazareth. James' experience was different again in the uniqueness of having been the brother of Jesus. But, in the account in Acts 15, we are shown how these very unique qualities can be blended in common mission.

Much about the early years and family life of Jesus remains unknown. We do know that He had brothers and sisters. We know that Joseph and Mary journeyed to Jerusalem from Galilee when Jesus was twelve years of age. We also read the story of His mother's consternation over His "unusual behavior" when He was in the synagogue with the elders and how He, in essence, said, "Don't you know that I am being who I am made to be—about My Father's business?" We know that Jesus was a carpenter who worked with Joseph in the carpenter trade. We also have several references during Jesus' ministry to His father, Joseph, as well as to His mother and siblings.

From Jesus' teaching we know that He understood the Scriptures quite well. Evidently He had a good synagogue education. We also know from His stories that He understood nature and the natural setting in Galilee. In addition, we are impressed that God chose to have His Son grow up in Galilee of the Nations, the part of the land that was much more diverse than Jerusalem, where about one third of the population was Jewish and the other two thirds primarily Roman and Greek. Galilee was the more cosmopolitan community, for the highways of the world from West to East, and North to South passed through Galilee. Jesus had a strong family life, so close that when His ministry raised questions, His mother and brothers came to call Him home.

In this brief review we discover that Jesus had a very strong and wholesome self-image, as well as a clear sense of God's work in His life. We learn from His life as well as His words what it meant for Him to respect His family, while walking responsibly before God in His mission. The Christian family has the special challenge of preparing children to "walk softly before the Lord" with a strong sense of security in being persons called of God.

There is a special place for self-fulfillment. But with this uniqueness there can still be a commonality of mission that unites a family in actualizing this diversity in the kingdom of Christ.

> Mission is purpose,
>   not a work somewhere out there,
>   not programs of action,
>   not orders of drivenness,
> But purpose as lifestyle.

> Mission is selfless,
>   not the extension of one's control,

> not the manipulation of others,
> not actions of aggression,
> But a giving of one's self to God.

For parents to look into the face of a newborn child and to know that this little one had a beginning with us, but will never end, is an awesome experience. The cradle and the grave are not the perimeters of life. We believe in resurrection, that 50 billion years from now we who walk with Christ will be unique persons living on with God! This faith-perspective gives greater dimension to our sense of uniqueness in role.

Our sharing together is intended to help each other fulfill the purpose of God in our lives. Dallas Willard, in *The Spirit of the Disciplines,* calls us to engage those disciplines which refine the life. He speaks of disciplines of abstinence and disciplines of engagement. By abstinence he means solitude, silence, fasting, frugality, chastity, secrecy, and sacrifice. By those of engagement he means study, worship, celebration, service, prayer, fellowship, and submission.

David Watson, speaking of the days before his operation for the cancer which took his life, said, "God's Word to us, especially His word spoken by His Spirit, through the Bible, is the very ingredient that feeds our faith." With this in mind, the family needs to encourage one another to feed on the Word regularly, to help each other to become robust spiritually.

To be fully unselfish, we need to translate the disciplines of life into mission. With the disclosure of God in Christ, we are able to order life in relation to the future. We know the future from the Christ event, the middle of history. We are now engaged in the kingdom that God is creating, as He is "calling out of the world a people for His name."

Accepting Diversity Brings Strength

Kingdom mission is global and yet cross-cultural in a given setting. The fulfillment of this mission calls for diversity in the community of faith. The family is the unit to engage this diversity. It is the primary social influence by which we extend Christ's mission into the marketplace of life. Our diversity is an asset, not a problem. We need to motivate families to recognize the strengths of diversity. As parents avoid trying to cast each child in the same mold, they will find that in the uniqueness of each member of the family there is an opening of another circle of life through which we can touch persons for Christ.

Paul wrote to Philemon about "the church that meets in your house" (v. 2). Just so, we in our time want to see the kingdom of God extended by families in every level of social experience. The Christian family will express what it means to be a people of God in any particular setting, in the growing global community at home.

This is one of the primary goals for excellence in education, the preparation of lives for loving service to our fellow beings. Knowledge without love leads to pride and separation from others, while knowledge with love has the power to enrich relationships. Knowledge, when acquired from a Christian perspective, will be matched with compassion. Floyd McClung has said, "People don't care how much we know until they know how much we care."

Families today, as never before in history, live as a part of the global village. This means that interracial and cross-cultural relationships are a very integral part of our lives. Families are the key to overcoming racism, prejudice, arrogance, and violence. We need to work together in a spirit of acceptance and affirmation that extends to all peoples.

There is no place in the Christian family for a mentality that judges and treats others as inferior because they are different. It is through the family that we can extend Jesus' teachings to love our neighbors as ourselves, and to love our enemies with a consistency that will show others how genuinely we care.

If we are truly evangelical, we will want to win every person to become a brother or sister in Christ. With such a faith we can never belittle another, minimize another's importance, or participate in war or violence that would take the life of one for whom Christ died. We will set all of our relationships in context with the mission of Christ, a mission of reconciliation. Wherever the Gospel is fully understood, people of faith will always "beat their swords into plowshares and their spears into pruning hooks" (Isaiah 2:4).

Esther was born of missionary parents in India. Her family includes three brothers, each in ministry: one ministers as a medical doctor, one as a pastor, and one has served with his wife for over forty years in Bihar, India. The sense of missions has been very central in our lives. Myron's family of six has four of the sons in the ministry. However, our immediate family has parried the social pressure from others on our children, as through the years the children faced the constant question, "Are you going to be a preacher like your dad? Or a missionary?" The answer that became almost ingrained was, "No, I'm going to be myself." The result has been a social worker, a businessman/pilot, and a teacher/lawyer, which is good. They can be a presence for Christ in those roles, just as much as we parents seek to be in our kind of ministries.

Each has a deep sense of mission to meet human need. They are not called to be preachers, but to live the Gospel in its regenerating and humanizing power. In many ways we share a similar mission, but with different roles or callings. We are, in different ways, laborers together with Christ.

In the midst of our Western individualism, and the rise of an "America first" attitude, we need to be reminded of the words of George Washington, "Observe good faith and justice toward all nations; cultivate peace and harmony with all." In the spirit of authentic mission as family, we pray that the next generation will measure their lives not by how many serve them, but by how many they serve.

Service Is a Spirit of Life That Is Not Seeking Power

Service is a spirit of life before it is an activity. This spirit is modeled in family as we serve one another in love. The disciplines by which we achieve a meaningful and rewarding family relationship provide the basis for extending these values to others.

It is not the differences between people that create problems, but the indifference. When we seek to live by the Spirit of Jesus, we will recognize His call to service. As Leo Tolstoy said, "The sole meaning of life is to serve humanity."

The spiritual vision of parents will be caught in some measure by their children. As the Prophet Joel said years before the occasion of the coming of the Spirit, and as quoted by Peter in his sermon on that day of Pentecost, "I will pour out My Spirit on all people. Your sons and daughters will prophesy, your young men will see visions, and your old men will dream dreams" (Acts 2:17).

As we grow older, our vision should be clearer and our priorities more singular. On this point, the late Orrie O. Miller, when an aged churchman in our denomination, was asked what he did with his vacation time, he replied, "I catch up on my pondering!" Being an old man, he was still dreaming dreams! And they were powerful dreams which live on today in the Mennonite Central Committee Relief service.

Dreaming dreams doesn't imply living in the past, retreating to yesteryear. Rather it is the projection of past and proven meanings into the present and the future. It was Pat Boone who said, "Today is unique. Don't let its wonderful moments go by unnoticed—and unused."

We Live Together in Grace

We are called as family to experience the grace of God together, to joy in his forgiveness and acceptance. Of course, there have been failures, things to forgive. But God acted in Christ to pay the price to forgive us. Just as He will bear the scars of His love forever, so He gives us grace to bear scars of love. And children often bear them for their parents, as well as parents bearing scars for their children.

There is a moving verse by Andrew Gillis that Myron frequently quotes in sermons on the family, that expresses this thought.

> Last night my little boy confessed to me,
>   Some childish wrong;
>   And kneeling at my knee
>   He prayed with tears—
>   "Dear God, make me a man
>   Like Daddy—wise and strong;
>   I know you can."
>
> Then while he slept,
>   I knelt beside his bed,
>   Confessed my sins,
>   And prayed with low-bowed head.
>   "O God, make me a child,
>   Like my child here—
>   Pure, guileless,
>   Trusting Thee with faith sincere.[4]

Epilogue

With the awareness that our achievements are very limited and our family is always in process, we submit ourselves to the transforming power of divine grace. We, parents and children, continue to accept, forgive, love, and grow together.

There is a line in Scripture which says, "A little child shall lead them." It would seem that while we learn from the simple love of the child, the childlike spirit of humility is a calling that comes to each of us.

Family is where we most realistically experience the meaning of grace. In fact, it may well be that God has so structured this social unit that our mistakes are set in the context of love, where the grace of forgiveness is the one power that binds us together. Here we see lived out day by day the very dynamic of saving grace that is known in God's forgiveness.

Thinking back over our respective families of origin, both of us can share highpoints of influence in the worship experiences we knew as family. It is not that some of the occasions of family prayer were not routine, but rather that when there were difficult times, the prayers of parents were the highest expression of their dependence upon God. Family life sets worship in a daily and an authentic context of life being lived in relation to our Lord.

There is a song known as the "family hymn" in many of our homes within the Mennonite community. It was written in 1890 by a man from our tradition, Amos Herr, and is based on Psalm 59:16, "I will sing of Your strength, I will

sing of Your love in the morning." It has for a century been
a family expression of worship together.

> I owe the Lord a morning song
> Of gratitude and praise,
> For the kind mercy He has shown
> In lengthening out my days.
>
> He kept me safe another night;
> I see another day;
> Now may His Spirit, as the light,
> Direct me in His way.
>
> Keep me from danger and from sin;
> Help me Thy will to do,
> So that my heart be pure within,
> And I Thy goodness know.
>
> Keep me till Thou wilt call me hence,
> Where never night can be;
> And save me, Lord, for Jesus' sake,
> He shed His blood for me.

Our sense of joy in the Lord, of dependence on Him, of
security in His love, gives us in turn a sense of mission to
share this spiritual reality with others. As Paul wrote, we are
Christ's "ambassadors" (2 Corinthians 5:19), agents of reconciliation. To us is committed the message and the ministry of
reconciliation. This is a commission that will involve the totality of our lives. Sharing faith authentically is a lifestyle.

Family is a seminary of life. It is a preparation to be God's
agents of reconciling love in a very troubled world. Ours is a
mission of Shalom, of love and wholeness. No unit can be
more authentically involved in this mission than the Christian
family. We are called to live the Gospel, to be a presence for
Christ in society. Saint Francis once said, "Preach the Gospel
in everything that you do. If necessary, use words!"

Endnotes

Chapter 1

1. M. Scott Peck, *The Road Less Traveled* (New York: A Touchstone Book, 1978), 12.
2. Stanley Hauerwas, *Christian Existence Today* (Durham, North Carolina: The Labyrinth Press, 1988), 92.

Chapter 2

1. Mike Mason, *The Mystery of Marriage* (Portland: Multnomah, 1985), 59.
2. David Augsburger, *Pastoral Counseling across Cultures* (Philadelphia: Westminster, 1986), 210.
3. Merton and Irene Strommen, *Five Cries of Parents* (San Francisco: Harper, 1985), 2, 4.
4. *USA TODAY,* 6 February 1992.
5. Mike Mason, *The Mystery of Marriage,* 59.
6. Ibid.
7. Harry Covert, Used with permission.

Chapter 3

1. (Scottdale, Pennsylvania: Herald Press, 1985), 54–55.
2. Gibson Winter, *Love and Conflict* (New York: Doubleday, 1958), 23.
3. Ibid., 55.
4. Ibid., 70.
5. Lois Wyse, *Love Poems for the Very Married* (New York: Harper & Row Publishers, Inc., 1967), 41.
6. Mike Mason, *The Mystery of Marriage* (Portland: Multnomah, 1985), 76.

7. M. Scott Peck, *The Road Less Traveled* (New York: A Touchstone Book, 1978), 300.

Chapter 4
1. Dietrich Bonhoeffer, *Creation and Fall* (London: SCM Press, 1959), 60.
2. Colleen and Louis Evans, Jr., *Bold Commitment* (Wheaton: Victor Books, 1983), 74.
3. Merton and Irene Strommen, *Five Cries of Parents* (San Francisco: Harper, 1985), 107.
4. Dietrich Bonhoeffer, *Creation and Fall*, 61.
5. Steve Garber, Used by permission.

Chapter 5
1. Merton and Irene Strommen, *Five Cries of Parents* (San Francisco: Harper, 1985), 9.
2. For more on forgiveness, see Myron's book, *The Peacemaker* (Nashville: Abindgon, 1987).
3. Gordon MacDonald, "How to Experience Forgiveness from the Heart," *Christian Herald*, March/April 1991, 17–18.
4. Ibid., 18.
5. A. Don Augsburger, *Marriages That Work* (Scottdale, Pennsylvania: Herald Press, 1984), 71–72.
6. M. Scott Peck, *The Road Less Traveled* (New York: A Touchstone Book, 1978), 22–23.

Chapter 6
1. M. Scott Peck, *The Road Less Traveled* (New York: A Touchstone Book, 1978), 24.
2. John Bradshaw, *The Family, A Revolutionary Way of Self-Discovery* (Deerfield Beach, Florida: Health Communications, 1988), 53–54.
3. John and Naomi Lederach, "Bill of Rights for Parents" (Mount Gretna, Pennsylvania: Philhaven Press, 1989). Used by permission.
4. M.Scott Peck, *The Road Less Traveled*, 99.

Chapter 7
1. M. Scott Peck, *The Road Less Traveled* (New York: A Touchstone Book, 1978), 24.
2. Catherine Marshall, *A Man Called Peter* (Greenwich, Connecticut: Pawcatt Publications, Inc., 1951), 142.

3. Merton and Irene Strommen, *Five Cries of Parents* (San Francisco: Harper, 1985), 163.

Chapter 8

1. Gloria Gaither, *What My Parents Did Right* (Nashville: Star Song, 1991), 36.
2. E. Stanley Jones, *Mastery* (Nashville: Abingdon, 1955), 338.
3. Jim Fairfield, September/October 1991, 22.
4. M. Scott Peck, *The Road Less Traveled* (New York: A Touchstone Book, 1978), 30,
5. Frontier Magazine Winter 1976.
6. "Every Grain of Sand," written by Bob Dylan © 1981 by Special Rider Music. All rights reserved. Used by permission.

Chapter 9

1. John Bradshaw, *The Family: A Revolutionary Way of Self-Discovery* (Deerfield Beach, Florida: Health Communications, 1988), 1.
2. Merton and Irene Strommen, *Five Cries of Parents* (San Francisco: Harper, 1985), 33.
3. Malcolm Muggeridge, *Confessions of a Twentieth Century Pilgrim* (New York: Harper & Row, 1988), 48.
4. John Bradshaw, *The Family*, 5.
5. Merton and Irene Strommen, *Five Cries of Parents*.
6. John Bradshaw, *The Family*, 5.
7. A. Don Augsburger, *Marriages That Work* (Scottdale, Pennsylvania: Herald Press, 1984), 25.
8. Merton and Irene Strommen, *Five Cries of Parents*, 37.
9. E. Stanley Jones, *Mastery* (Nashville: Abingdon, 1955), 337.
10. *The Marketplace* (Winnepeg, Manitoba: Mennonite Economic Development Association), 21.
11. *Masterpieces of Religious Verse* (New York: Harper and Brothers, 1948), 361.

Chapter 10

1. Virginia Satir, Taken from an article in *The Washington Post.*
2. John Bradshaw, *The Family: A Revolutionary Way of Self-Discovery* (Deerfield Beach, Florida: Health Communications, 1988), 48–49.
3. *Masterpieces of Religious Verse* (New York: Harper and Brothers, 1948), 93.
4. Ibid. 383.